NUTRI
NINJA 2-in-1

Healthy & Delicious
Made Easy

150 Recipes from healthy nutrient-rich juices to delicious meal making

Nutritional Analyses: Calculations for the nutritional analyses in this book are based on the largest number of servings listed within the recipes. Calculations are rounded up to the nearest gram or milligram, as appropriate.
If two options for an ingredient are listed, the first one is used.
Not included are optional ingredients or serving suggestions.

Editors and Content: Katie Barry, Jane Lo, Reggie Macon, Bob Warden

Recipe Development: Donna Scocozza, Culinary Director, The Euro-Pro Culinary Innovation Team and Great Flavors Recipe Development Team

Graphic Designer: Leslie Anne Feagley

Creative/Photo Director: Keith Manning

Photography: Quentin Bacon and Gary Sloan

Published in the United States of America by

Great Flavors LLC
P.O. Box 250
New Hope, PA 18938

ISBN: 978-1-4951-3688-7

10   9   8   7   6   5   4   3   2   1

Printed in China

table of contents

Your Nutri Ninja® 2-in-1

The Nutri Ninja® 2-in-1 combines multiple kitchen appliances into one easy-to-use compact kitchen system. The 40-ounce Processor Bowl simplifies meal prep, making it fast and easy to create nutritious meals and beverages with minimal cleanup. Use the 16-ounce Nutri-Ninja® Cup to create super food juices, salad dressings, and sauces in seconds.

The Nutri Ninja® 2-in-1 power pod to prep ingredients for meal making in the 40-ounce Processor Bowl or flip the pod over to make nutritious single-serve drinks. The results? A powerful go-to kitchen tool for creating easy and delicious, healthy meals!

New to this? We've got you covered. Choose any of our delicious recipes. Plus, we have helpful tips and charts to customize your own!

Our recipes include:

- high-nutrient, low-starch vegetables
- lower-sugar fruits
- detoxifying herbs
- forward-thinking, super-food ingredients

To support your healthier lifestyle, we've identified key foods that can help to deliver specific health-enhancing benefits. Helpful tips from our registered dietitians and nutritionists teach you about basic nutrient extract juicing. It couldn't be easier—your daily dose of vegetables and fruits is just a few sips away.

why nutrient extract?

Nutrient extract juices provide you with a simple way to get your daily recommended nutritional intake. Key benefits include:

- Good source of nutrition— easy way to get your daily servings of fruits and vegetables
- Great variety of ingredients, textures, and flavor options
- A quick and easy meal replacement
- Easy additions of protein and "good fats"
- Adds fiber to your diet

healthy swaps

Use this guide to see how you can make simple ingredient substitutions that will give your recipes a healthy boost.

	INSTEAD OF	SUBSTITUTE WITH THIS
DAIRY	Sour cream, full-fat	Plain low-fat yogurt, plain Greek yogurt
	Milk, evaporate	Evaporated skim milk
	Whole milk	1% milk, nonfat milk, almond milk
	Cheddar cheese	Low-fat cheddar cheese
	Ice cream	Frozen yogurt or sorbet
	Cream cheese	Neufchâtel or light cream cheese
	Whipped cream	Light whipped topping
	Ricotta cheese	Low-fat ricotta cheese
	Cream	Fat-free half & half, evaporated skim milk
	Yogurt, fruit-flavored	Plain yogurt with fresh fruit slices
PROTEIN	Bacon	Canadian bacon, turkey bacon, smoked turkey, or lean prosciutto (Italian ham)
	Ground beef	Extra-lean or lean ground beef, ground chicken or turkey breast, tofu, tempeh
	Meat as the main ingredient	Three times as many vegetables as the meat on pizzas or in casseroles, soups, and stews
	Eggs	Two egg whites or ¼ cup egg substitute for each whole egg
OTHER	Soups, creamed	Nonfat, milk-based soups, puréed carrots, potatoes, or tofu for thickening agents
	Soups, sauces, dressings, crackers, or canned meat, fish, or vegetables	Low-sodium or reduced-sodium versions

healthy swaps

	INSTEAD OF	SUBSTITUTE WITH THIS
GRAINS	Bread, white	Whole-grain bread
	Bread crumbs, dry	Crushed bran cereal or almond meal
	Pasta, enriched (white)	Whole wheat pasta
	Rice, white	Brown rice, wild rice, bulgur, or pearl barley
FAT	Butter, margarine, shortening, or oil in baked goods	Applesauce or prune purée for half of the called-for butter, shortening, or oil; butter spreads or shortenings specially formulated for baking that don't have trans fats (Note: To avoid dense, soggy, or flat baked goods, don't substitute oil for butter or shortening. Also don't substitute diet, whipped, or tub-style margarine for regular margarine.)
	Butter, margarine, shortening, or oil to prevent sticking	Cooking spray or nonstick pans
	Mayonnaise	Reduced-calorie mayonnaise-type salad dressing or reduced-calorie, reduced-fat mayonnaise
	Oil-based marinades	Wine, balsamic vinegar, fruit juice, or nonfat broth
SUGAR	Sugar	In most baked goods you can reduce the amount of sugar by one-half; intensify sweetness by adding vanilla, nutmeg, or cinnamon.
	Syrup	Puréed fruit, such as applesauce, or low-calorie, sugar-free syrup
	Chocolate chips	Craisins
SAUCES	Soy sauce	Low-sodium soy sauce, tamari sauce (gluten-free!), hot mustard sauce
SALT	Salt	Herbs, spices, citrus juices (lemon, lime, orange), rice vinegar, salt-free seasoning mixes or herb blends, low-sodium soy sauce (cuts the sodium in half by equal volume while boosting flavor)
	Seasoning salt, such as garlic salt, celery salt, or onion salt	Herb-only seasonings, such as garlic powder, celery seed or onion flakes. Finely chopped herbs, garlic, celery, or onions.

super food ingredients

Liven up the flavor and boost the nutritional value of any recipe in this book with these healthy bonus add-ins!

Bonus Ingredient	Characteristics
Açaí	• Unique, complex blend of essential fats, antioxidants, amino acids, and calcium • Available in powder and frozen concentrate; has a berry flavor without sweetness
Aloe Vera Juice	• Can serve as a way of cleansing the body of toxins • Features a bright, refreshing flavor
Basil	• Contains micronutrients, such as manganese and copper, providing antioxidant properties • Fragrant, large leaf herb tastes great with other greens and strawberries
Chia Seeds	• A total package with protein, fiber, calcium and omega-3 fats that can help with regularity and weight management • Easily absorbs liquids, making drinks thicker, with a slightly nutty taste
Cilantro	• An excellent detoxifier that binds heavy metals, helping to eliminate toxins from the body • Delicate leaf herb that pairs well with vegetables and fruits including avocado and tomato
Cinnamon	• Pairs well with nut milks, raisins, dates and winter fruits and vegetables
Coconut Oil	• Contains medium-chain triglycerides, which can promote the burning of fat • Adds a smoothness to blended drinks and keeps you feeling full
Flax seeds	• Contains lignin, a class of phytoestrogens considered to have antioxidant properties • Grind seeds well to release nutrients or use ground flax; store in the refrigerator after grinding or opening

Bonus Ingredient	Characteristics
Ginger	• An anti-inflammatory plant root that can aid the immune system and help quell nausea
Goji Berries	• A concentrated source of amino acids and antioxidants that may help support the immune system • Provide a hint of sweetness and texture to food. Available as dried berries
Hemp Seeds	• Packed with protein, iron, and vitamin E • The slightly nutty flavor goes will with vegetables or fruits
Maca	• An adaptogen that can regulate mood, energy levels, and support a healthy libido • Expect a bland cocoa flavor with a hint of sweetness
Mint	• An herb that promotes beneficial enzymes that can help soothe the digestive tract • Has a cool minty flavor that complements several types of fruits
Parsley	• Offers great antioxidant support and high in flavonoids and vitamins A & C • Not only a garnish, it's a great additive for green drinks
Pomegranate Juice	• A play of antioxidants—anthocyanins, tannins, ellagic acid—for immune system and blood pressure support • Intensely flavored as a juice or concentrate; Pairs well with berries and chocolate
Turmeric	• Contains Curcumin, an active component that supports joint health and cardiovascular function • Pairs well with carrots, sweet potatoes
Tart Cherry Juice	• Contains phytonutrients that help reduce inflammation, exercise recovery, and improve sleep

sugar + fiber in fruits & vegetables

The sugar and fiber content of fruits and vegetables can be helpful when deciding which foods to use in your drinks, particularly if you're concerned about weight loss. The following charts reflect the fruits and vegetables used in our recipes. Listed according to sugar content, from lowest to highest value, the following charts also provide the corresponding fiber content. The values indicated are for typical serving sizes of each food. For items indicating "1" piece, the fruits are medium in size.

Try to avoid added sugars in your diet, which are found in processed foods. Instead, get your sugar from naturally occurring sources, such as fruits and vegetables. Along with natural sugar, nature packages fruits and vegetables with fiber, vitamins, minerals, and antioxidants—what you need for vibrant health.

Moderate Sugar Content Foods

FOOD	SERVING SIZE	SUGAR (GRAMS)	FIBER (GRAMS)
Sweet potato	1 cup	6	4
Blackberries	1 cup	7	8
Strawberries	1 cup	7	3
Beets	1 cup	9	4
Grapefruit	1	9	1
Tangerine	1	9	2
Watermelon	1 cup	9	1

Low Sugar Content Foods

FOOD	SERVING SIZE	SUGAR (GRAMS)	FIBER (GRAMS)
Cilantro	1 cup	0	1
Spinach	1 cup	0	1
Dandelion greens	1 cup	0	2
Swiss chard	1 cup	0	1
Romaine	1 cup	1	1
Watercress	1 cup	1	0
Parsley	1 cup	1	2
Celery	1	1	1
Bok choy	1 cup	1	1
Kale	1 cup	1	2
Lime	1 cup	1	2
Avocado	1 cup	1	10
Kiwi	1	2	6
Lemon	1	2	2
Cabbage	1 cup	3	2
Goji berries	2 tbsp.	4	1
Tomato	1 cup	5	2
Coconut	1 cup	5	7
Pepper	1	5	3
Raspberries	1 cup	5	8

customize your own

Get creative with your Ninja®, and customize a healthy blend of your very own! Don't be afraid to experiment. Check out our suggestions below for creating your own signature nutrient extract juice!

To Make It Thicker

Try adding one of these ingredients for a creamier drink and to boost your nutritional intake:
- ¼ ripe banana
- 2 tablespoons avocado
- ½ tablespoon chia seeds

HOW TO MAKE A CHIA GEL: Combine 4 tablespoons of chia seeds with 2 cups of water or another liquid like coconut water. After 10 to 15 minutes, you'll have a gel! Use 1 or 2 tablespoons of gel to thicken drinks to your desired consistency. Cover and refrigerate for up to one week.

To Make It Thinner

The thickness of blended drinks depends on ice usage and whether the ingredients are fresh or frozen. To regulate the consistency of your smoothies and beverages, you can add one of these healthful ingredients to thin it down:

- 2 tablespoons green tea or chamomile tea
- 2 tablespoons coconut water
- Add a small amount of a high-moisture food, such as celery, lettuce, cucumber, lemon or lime
- Add water—important to rehydrate!
- Unsweetened almond milk adds richness, great with tropical fruits!

To Make It Sweeter

The recipes in this book are created with ingredients that are naturally low in sugar. If your taste buds require beverages that are a little sweeter, we recommend using the ingredients below.

- 1 teaspoon agave
- 1 date
- 1½ teaspoons honey
- 1½ teaspoons maple syrup
- ½ packet stevia

powerful combinations

Sometimes using ingredients together delivers a bigger nutritional benefit than consuming them individually. Here are a few go-together ideas for creating your own drinks that will complement your healthy eating efforts.

- Full-fat coconut milk or coconut oil + turmeric =
  Better utilization of turmeric's potent antioxidant compound, Curcumin, aided by the fat in coconut

- Citrus + dark leafy greens =
  Optimal absorption of the iron in greens with the help of vitamin C–rich citrus

- Avocado or nuts + tomatoes or watermelon =
  Enhanced absorption of lycopene—the red-colored antioxidant—with the assistance of the healthy fats in avocado or nuts

- Kale or Swiss chard + strawberries =
  Higher availability of B vitamins found in leafy greens along with the vitamin C in berries

- Sweet potatoes or carrots + nuts =
  Improved absorption of fat-soluble vitamin A, contained in many orange foods, possible with the help of the healthy fats in nuts

Mix & Match Recipe Ideas

Create your own nutrient-rich juices or healthy smoothies with these great food and flavor combos!

THESE TASTE GREAT	WITH ANY OF THESE
apples, pears, nut milks	cinnamon, nutmeg, almonds, walnuts
kale, Swiss chard, romaine	fresh lemons, pears, kiwi, ginger
green tea	all berries, tart cherry and pomegranate concentrates
sweet potatoes, carrots, butternut squash	turmeric, maple syrup
arugula	mint, pears, apples
pineapple, mango, papaya	coconut, bananas
strawberries	basil, mint, goji berries

PREP TIME: 5 minutes   MAKES: 1 serving   CONTAINER: 16-ounce Nutri Ninja® Cup

island mood boost

This drink is specially designed to give you a nice, prolonged energy release through-out the day.

ingredients

½ cup frozen mango chunks

1 cup coconut water

½ cup fresh pineapple chunks

½ small banana

½ cup frozen strawberries

1 teaspoon flax seed

directions

1. Place all ingredients into the 16-ounce Nutri Ninja® Cup in the order listed.

2. BLEND until smooth.

PREP TIME: 5 minutes   MAKES: 1 serving   CONTAINER: 16-ounce Nutri Ninja® Cup

pineapple pleaser

The combination of pineapple and papaya makes for a nutrient-dense drink high in vitamin C.

ingredients

¾ cup frozen pineapple chunks

2 teaspoons cashew butter

¾ cup rice milk

½ cup fresh, ripe papaya chunks

directions

1. Place all ingredients into the 16-ounce Nutri Ninja® Cup in the order listed.

2. BLEND until smooth.

NINJA
KNOW-HOW

SUBSTITUTE HAZELNUT MILK WITH ALMOND MILK IF PREFERRED.

PREP TIME: 5 minutes   MAKES: 2 servings   CONTAINER: 40-ounce Processor Bowl

avocado-lada

This drink is creamy and delicious; the coconut water gives it a tropical flavor. Plus, it's a great fiber boost.

ingredients

1 ripe avocado pitted, quartered, peeled

1 small banana

1½ cups coconut water

1 cup frozen pineapple chunks

directions

1. Place all ingredients into the 40-ounce Processor Bowl in the order listed.

2. BLEND until smooth.

 NINJA KNOW-HOW   YOU CAN SUBSTITUTE COCONUT MILK FOR A RICHER ENERGY BOOST.

PREP TIME: 5 minutes   MAKES: 1 serving   CONTAINER: 16-ounce Nutri Ninja® Cup

kick-start my day

A perfect protein morning starter.

ingredients

¾ cup frozen strawberries

¼ small banana

¾ cup orange juice

1 tablespoon vanilla protein powder

directions

1. Place all ingredients into the 16-ounce Nutri Ninja® Cup in the order listed.

2. BLEND until smooth.

PREP TIME: 5 minutes   MAKES: 1 serving   CONTAINER: 16-ounce Nutri Ninja® Cup

kale me up

A great detoxifying drink whenever you feel burnt out and need a pick-me-up.

ingredients

½ cup ice

1 cup water

½ cup green seedless grapes

¼ cup English cucumber

½ cup loosely packed kale leaves

¼ apple, cored

directions

1. Place all ingredients into the 16-ounce Nutri Ninja® Cup in the order listed.

2. BLEND until smooth.

NINJA
KNOW-HOW

SUBSTITUTE PINEAPPLE JUICE FOR WATER FOR EXTRA SWEETNESS.

PREP TIME: 5 minutes MAKES: 1 serving CONTAINER: 16-ounce Nutri Ninja® Cup

spicy pineapple recharge

Sweet, tangy, and spicy, this drink is truly a party in a glass.

ingredients

¼ cup ice

¼ small jalapeño pepper, seeded

¼-inch piece fresh ginger, peeled

¼ lime, peeled, seeded

1 cup fresh pineapple chunks

⅓ cup orange juice

directions

1. Place all ingredients into the 16-ounce Nutri Ninja® Cup in the order listed.
2. BLEND until smooth.

PREP TIME: 5 minutes   MAKES: 1 serving   CONTAINER: 16-ounce Nutri Ninja® Cup

top of the class

Just like pumpkin pie, but light and nourishing. Maple syrup is a healthier alternative as a sweetener. The flax seeds and cabbage provide fiber.

ingredients

½ cup ice

1 cup water

2 teaspoons flax seeds

1 tablespoon maple syrup

¼-inch piece fresh ginger, peeled

¼ apple, cored

¼ cup canned pumpkin purée

½ cup chopped green cabbage

directions

1. Place all ingredients into the 16-ounce Nutri Ninja® Cup in the order listed.

2. BLEND until smooth.

NINJA KNOW-HOW USE BROCCOLI SPROUTS IN PLACE OF CABBAGE. ONE TABLESPOON BROCCOLI SPROUTS CONTAINS THE EQUIVALENT MICRONUTRIENT CONTENT OF A POUND OF RAW BROCCOLI.

PREP TIME: 5 minutes   MAKES: 1 serving   CONTAINER: 16-ounce Nutri Ninja® Cup

chocolate almond fusion

Unsweetened cocoa powder is a great ingredient to add indulgence, especially when combined with the flavors of almond and banana.

ingredients

½ cup ice

¾ cup almond milk

1 teaspoon agave nectar

1 tablespoon almond butter

2 teaspoons unsweetened cocoa powder

1 small banana

½ cup loosely packed kale leaves

directions

1. Place all ingredients into the 16-ounce Nutri Ninja® Cup in the order listed.

2. BLEND until smooth.

NINJA
KNOW-HOW

ADD 1 TABLESPOON CACAO POWDER FOR A SUPER FOOD BOOST.

PREP TIME: 5 minutes   MAKES: 4 servings   CONTAINER: 40-ounce Processor Bowl

peach soother smoothie

Peaches, pears, and yogurt pair perfectly with ginger in this smoother loaded with probiotics.

ingredients

¼-inch piece fresh ginger, peeled

1½ pears, quartered, cored

2 tablespoons ground flax seeds

1½ cups plain, nonfat kefir

¾ cup nonfat yogurt

1¼ cups frozen peach slices

directions

1. Place all ingredients into the 40-ounce Processor Bowl in the order listed.

2. BLEND until smooth.

NINJA KNOW-HOW — ADD AN EXTRA TABLESPOON OF FLAX SEEDS FOR EXTRA FIBER.

frozen kale cacao

Known as the "queen of greens", kale is recognized for its exceptional nutrient richness, many health benefits, and delicious flavor.

ingredients

¼ cup ice

½ cup packed kale leaves

1 small frozen banana, quartered

2 pitted dates

1 teaspoon unsweetened cocoa powder

1 scoop chocolate protein powder

1¼ cups unsweetened coconut milk

directions

1. Place all ingredients into the 16-ounce Nutri Ninja® Cup in the order listed.

2. BLEND until smooth.

PREP TIME: 5 minutes MAKES: 1 serving CONTAINER: 16-ounce Nutri Ninja® Cup

beet & go

A healthy drinkable salad that tastes wonderful. Both the beets and Swiss chard help reduce cholesterol and clear toxins from your system.

ingredients

½ cup ice

1 cup water

½ small carrot, peeled, halved

¼ apple, cored

¼-inch piece fresh ginger, peeled

¼ cup swiss chard leaves

½ cup cooked beets

directions

1. Place all ingredients into the 16-ounce Nutri Ninja® Cup in the order listed.

2. BLEND until smooth.

 NINJA KNOW-HOW ADD APPLE CIDER VINEGAR OR BLACK PEPPER.

PREP TIME: 5 minutes   MAKES: 2 servings   CONTAINER: 40-ounce Processor Bowl

cashew honey nectar smoothie

A delicious sweet potato casserole with the heart-healthy benefit of cashews and unique flavor of nutmeg.

ingredients

1 cup cooked sweet potato

¼ cup cashews

3 tablespoons honey

½ teaspoon ground nutmeg

2¼ cups pear nectar

¾ cup nonfat yogurt

directions

1. Place all ingredients into the 40-ounce Processor Bowl in the order listed.

2. BLEND until smooth.

NINJA
KNOW-HOW

ALWAYS GRIND NUTMEG
FRESH JUST AS YOU
ARE READY TO USE IT.

PREP TIME: 5 minutes   MAKES: 2 servings   CONTAINER: 40-ounce Processor Bowl

super berry recovery

Fat free, and rich in potassium & Vitamin C, this berry blast is perfect for hydrating after your workout!

ingredients

1 cup red seedless grapes

½ apple, cored, halved

2 tablespoons vanilla protein powder

¾ cup coconut water

1¼ cups frozen blueberries

directions

1. Place all ingredients into the 40-ounce Processor Bowl in the order listed.

2. BLEND until smooth.

 KNOW-HOW DON'T CONFUSE COCONUT WATER WITH COCONUT MILK. COCONUT WATER IS A CLEAR LIQUID IN THE FRUIT'S CENTER THAT IS TAPPED FROM YOUNG, GREEN COCONUTS.

PREP TIME: 5 minutes   MAKES: 4 servings   CONTAINER: 40-ounce Processor Bowl

tropical squeeze smoothie

A delicious tropical yogurt smoothie, perfect as a mid-morning or afternoon pick-me-up.

ingredients

1 small banana

1 orange, peeled, quartered

½ cup fresh pineapple chunks

2 cups water

1 cup nonfat yogurt

1¼ cups frozen mango chunks

directions

1. Place all ingredients into the 40-ounce Processor Bowl in the order listed.

2. BLEND until smooth.

NINJA KNOW-HOW — LOOK FOR A PINEAPPLE THAT IS HEAVY FOR ITS SIZE. ALSO LOOK FOR A SWEET, FRAGRANT SMELL AT THE STEM END.

PREP TIME: 5 minutes   MAKES: 2 servings   CONTAINER: 40-ounce Processor Bowl

watermelon quench

A wonderfully refreshing source of lycopene, watermelon is loaded with phytonutrients that boast heart and bone health.

ingredients

1½ cups watermelon chunks

1 cup pomegranate juice

½ cup frozen peach slices

directions

1. Place all ingredients into the 40-ounce Processor Bowl in the order listed.

2. BLEND until smooth.

NINJA KNOW-HOW

PHYTONUTRIENTS REACH THEIR PEAK IN RIPE FRUIT, AND THIS IS ESPECIALLY TRUE FOR WATERMELON.

PREP TIME: 5 minutes   MAKES: 1 serving   CONTAINER: 16-ounce Nutri Ninja® Cup

lean green ninja

Not only a green smoothie that's bursting with vitamin C, the tropical fruit flavors mask the greens, making it simply delicious!

ingredients

¼ cup ice

¼ cup coconut water

½ small banana

¼ cup fresh mango chunks

¼ cup fresh pineapple chunks

¼ cup loosely packed kale leaves

¼ cup loosely packed baby spinach

directions

1. Place all ingredients into the 16-ounce Nutri Ninja® Cup in the order listed.

2. BLEND until smooth.

 NINJA KNOW-HOW   ADD 1 OR 2 TABLESPOONS FLAX SEEDS FOR AN ADDITIONAL FIBER BOOST.

PREP TIME: 5 minutes   MAKES: 2 servings   CONTAINER: 40-ounce Processor Bowl

the refueler

A perfect family smoothie to share after a good workout.

ingredients

1 orange, peeled, quartered

1 small banana

1 carrot, peeled, quartered

2 cups unsweetened almond milk

1 cup ice

directions

1. Place all ingredients into the 40-ounce Processor Bowl in the order listed.

2. BLEND until smooth.

NINJA KNOW-HOW CARROTS WITH A LARGER DIAMETER WILL BE SWEETER SINCE SUGARS ARE CONCENTRATED IN THE CORE.

PREP TIME: 5 minutes   MAKES: 1 serving   CONTAINER: 16-ounce Nutri Ninja® Cup

iced orange chocolate blast

Chocolate and orange are a perfect marriage of taste and nutrition.

ingredients

¼ cup ice

½ cup nonfat vanilla yogurt

¾ cup nonfat milk

¼ teaspoon ground cinnamon

1 teaspoon agave nectar

1 tablespoon unsweetened cocoa powder

1 seedless orange, peeled, quartered

directions

1. Place all ingredients into the 16-ounce Nutri Ninja® Cup in the order listed.

2. BLEND until smooth.

KNOW-HOW

ADD 2 TABLESPOONS CACAO NIBS FOR A SUPER FOOD BOOST. CONTAINS THE SAME BENEFITS OF DARK CHOCOLATE WITHOUT THE SUGAR.

PREP TIME: 5 minutes   MAKES: 2 servings   CONTAINER: 40-ounce Processor Bowl

vitamin c bomb

Big flavors of citrus are paired with cranberry and kiwi for a bright antioxidant wake-me-up and a great source of vitamin C.

ingredients

¼ grapefruit, peeled

½ orange, peeled

1 kiwi, peeled, halved

¼ cup loosely packed fresh parsley leaves

1½ cups cranberry juice

¾ cup ice

directions

1. Place all ingredients into the 40-ounce Processor Bowl in the order listed.

2. BLEND until smooth.

NINJA
KNOW-HOW
SWITCH UP THE CITRUS FRUITS TO YOUR LIKING—LOOK FOR DIFFERENT ORANGE AND GRAPEFRUIT VARIETIES!

PREP TIME: 5 minutes   MAKES: 2 servings   CONTAINER: 40-ounce Processor Bowl

citus spirulina blast

A fresh blast of citrus pumped up with a hint of spirulina rich in vitamins, minerals, and carotenoids.

ingredients

½ grapefruit, peeled, quartered

½ orange, peeled, quartered

¾ cup fresh pineapple chunks

1 teaspoon spirulina

⅛ cup lime juice

1 cup water

1 cup ice

directions

1. Place all ingredients into the 40-ounce Processor Bowl in the order listed.

2. BLEND until smooth.

NINJA KNOW-HOW

ADD 2 TABLESPOONS AÇAÍ POWDER FOR A SUPER FOOD BOOST.

PREP TIME: 5 minutes   MAKES: 1 serving   CONTAINER: 16-ounce Nutri Ninja® Cup

powerball

Blueberries are full of antioxidants and phytonutrients. Start your day off right with this luscious energy booster.

ingredients

¾ cup frozen blueberries

¾ cup unsweetened coconut milk

½ small banana

½ teaspoon unsweetened cocoa powder

directions

1. Place all ingredients into the 16-ounce Nutri Ninja® Cup in the order listed.

2. BLEND until smooth.

 NINJA KNOW-HOW | ADD 1 TABLESPOON MACA POWDER FOR A SUPER FOOD BOOST.

PREP TIME: 5 minutes   MAKES: 4 servings   CONTAINER: 40-ounce Processor Bowl

fruit salad smoothie

A perfect way to have a delicious fruit salad on the go, filled with Vitamin C and potassium!

ingredients

½ cup frozen pineapple chunks

¾ cup frozen mango chunks

1 cup green seedless grapes

1 small banana, halved

½ apple, peeled, cored, halved

1 cup orange juice

directions

1. Place all ingredients into the 40-ounce Processor Bowl in the order listed.

2. BLEND until smooth.

PREP TIME: 5 minutes   MAKES: 1 serving   CONTAINER: 16-ounce Nutri Ninja® Cup

peach yogurt smoothie

Peaches, pears, and yogurt pair perfectly with ginger in this smoother loaded with probiotics.

ingredients

½ cup frozen peach slices

⅛-inch piece fresh ginger, peeled

½ pear, cored, quartered

1 tablespoon ground flax seeds

¾ cup nonfat, plain kefir

¼ cup nonfat yogurt

directions

1. Place all ingredients into the 16-ounce Nutri Ninja® Cup in the order listed.

2. BLEND until smooth.

 NINJA KNOW-HOW ADD AN EXTRA TABLESOON OF FLAX SEEDS FOR EXTRA FIBER.

PREP TIME: 5 minutes   MAKES: 2 servings   CONTAINER: 40-ounce Processor Bowl

watermelon cooler

Freeze to a slightly slushy consistency for a low-calorie refreshing cleanser.

ingredients

¼ pear, cored

2 large fresh basil leaves

2 cups chilled watermelon chunks

directions

1. Place all ingredients into the 40-ounce Processor Bowl in the order listed.

2. BLEND until smooth.

NINJA KNOW-HOW ADD ⅛ TEASPOON HOLY BASIL POWDER, ALSO CALLED TULSI, FOR A SUPER FOOD BOOST.

PREP TIME: 5 minutes   MAKES: 4 servings   CONTAINER: 40-ounce Processor Bowl

strawberry banana

One of the most popular smoothies ordered in today's smoothie bars. It contains 6 grams of fiber, 8 grams of protein, and 160% of your daily vitamin C requirement.

ingredients

2 small bananas, halved

2 cups low-fat milk

¼ cup agave nectar

2 cups frozen strawberries

directions

1. Place all ingredients into the 40-ounce Processor Bowl in the order listed.

2. BLEND until smooth.

PREP TIME: 5 minutes   MAKES: 1 serving   CONTAINER: 16-ounce Nutri Ninja® Cup

call me popeye

Who knew green could be so yummy? A perfect smoothie filled with antioxidants!

ingredients

½ cup ice

⅔ cup hazelnut milk

½ cup loosely packed baby spinach

½ cup chopped green cabbage

½ ripe kiwi, peeled

½ celery stalk, halved

1 pitted date

directions

1. Place all ingredients into the 16-ounce Nutri Ninja® Cup in the order listed.

2. BLEND until smooth.

 NINJA KNOW-HOW

SUBSTITUTE HAZELNUT MILK FOR ALMOND MILK IF PREFERRED.

PREP TIME: 5 minutes   MAKES: 1 serving   CONTAINER: 16-ounce Nutri Ninja® Cup

citrus ginger support

Need a vitamin C boost? This delicious refresher contains 190% of your daily vitamin C requirement. Ginger is used not only as food, but also for its aromatic and many health promoting properties.

ingredients

½ cup frozen mango chunks

¼ cup ice

¼-inch piece fresh ginger, peeled

½ pink grapefruit, peeled, halved, seeded

½ seedless orange, peeled, halved

½ lime, peeled

directions

1. Place all ingredients into the 16-ounce Nutri Ninja® Cup in the order listed.

2. BLEND until smooth.

NINJA™
KNOW-HOW
ADD 2 TEASPOONS AÇAÍ POWDER FOR A SUPER FOOD BOOST.

PREP TIME: 5 minutes   MAKES: 1 serving   CONTAINER: 16-ounce Nutri Ninja® Cup

berry healthy

Spinach blends perfectly with the natural sweetness and flavor of the fruit. The kids will not know it's in there.

ingredients

¼ cup ice

¼ cup packed baby spinach

¼ cup water

¼ cup hulled strawberries

¼ cup blueberries

½ cup fresh mango chunks

¼ cup fresh fresh pineapple chunks

directions

1. Place all ingredients into the 16-ounce Nutri Ninja® Cup in the order listed.

2. BLEND until smooth.

NINJA KNOW-HOW ADD 1 TEASPOON FRESH GINGER FOR A SUPER FOOD BOOST.

PREP TIME: 5 minutes   MAKES: 1 serving   CONTAINER: 16-ounce Nutri Ninja® Cup

sweet spinach detox

The combination of citrus with greens will help with the absorption of iron, plus it's a great way to get spinach into your diet!

ingredients

¼ cup ice

⅓ cup packed baby spinach

¼-inch piece fresh ginger, peeled

¾ green apple, cored, quartered

¼ lemon, peeled, seeded

2 teaspoons agave nectar or honey

⅛ cup apple juice

⅛ cup water

directions

1. Place all ingredients into the 16-ounce Nutri Ninja® Cup in the order listed.

2. BLEND until smooth.

NINJA KNOW-HOW ADD ½ ORANGE TO ADD TO THE VITAMIN C PUNCH!

PREP TIME: 5 minutes   MAKES: 4–6 servings   CONTAINER: 40-ounce Processor Bowl

spiced cucumber

Just like a chilled summer soup, cooling and refreshing, and only 50 calories! The inside temperature of a cucumber can actually be up to 20% cooler than the outside.

ingredients

⅔ English cucumber, quartered

1¼ cups cantaloupe chunks

1 jalapeño, seeded

1 cup green seedless grapes

2 cups water

1¼ cups ice

directions

1. Place all ingredients into the 40-ounce Processor Bowl in the order listed.

2. BLEND until smooth.

NINJA KNOW-HOW — USE OTHER TYPES OF CUCUMBERS FOR VARIETY—THEY CAN BE WHITE, YELLOW, OR ORANGE, AND LONG, VERY SHORT, CURVED, STRAIGHT, OVAL, LEMON SHAPED, OR EVEN ROUND.

PREP TIME: 5 minutes   MAKES: 1 serving   CONTAINER: 16-ounce Nutri Ninja® Cup

super green smoothie

With only 70 calories, this tasty green smoothie is the perfect between-meal refresher.

ingredients

¼ cup ice

¼ cup packed baby spinach

1½-inch piece medium cucumber, peeled and cut lengthwise

6 seedless grapes

½ cup honeydew melon chunks

¼ orange, peeled, halved

directions

1. Place all ingredients into the 16-ounce Nutri Ninja® Cup in the order listed.

2. BLEND until smooth.

NINJA KNOW-HOW   ADD 1 TABLESPOON RAW PARSLEY FOR A SUPER FOOD BOOST.

PREP TIME: 5 minutes   MAKES: 1 serving   CONTAINER: 16-ounce Nutri Ninja® Cup

cool honeydew cleanser

This cool cucumber honeydew refresher is only 80 calories, the perfect stress reducer.

ingredients

¼ cup ice

¼ medium cucumber, peeled, halved

½ cup melon chunks

½ cup fresh pineapple chunks

¼ cup water

directions

1. Place all ingredients into the 16-ounce Nutri Ninja® Cup in the order listed.

2. BLEND until smooth.

NINJA KNOW-HOW ADD 2 TABLESPOONS TART CHERRY CONCENTRATE FOR A HIGH ANTIOXIDANT SUPER FOOD BOOST.

PREP TIME: 5 minutes   MAKES: 1 serving   CONTAINER: 16-ounce Nutri Ninja® Cup

veggie power

The vitamin C in the broccoli and tomatoes helps convert the iron in spinach into a form that is more available to the body.

ingredients

½ cup ice

¼ vine ripe tomato, halved

¼ cup loosely packed baby spinach

1 celery stalk, quartered

¼ cup broccoli florets

1 tablespoon fresh fresh basil leaves

¼ apple, cored

⅛ teaspoon ground black pepper

1 cup water

directions

1. Place all ingredients into the 16-ounce Nutri Ninja® Cup in the order listed.

2. BLEND until smooth.

NINJA KNOW-HOW — FOR A DELICIOUS TOPPER TRY SPRINKLING GARLIC POWDER ON TOP.

PREP TIME: 5 minutes   MAKES: 1 serving   CONTAINER: 16-ounce Nutri Ninja® Cup

mango crush

Mint ramps up the antioxidants. The mango and almond milk give this delicious drink a creamy texture without the cream. Mango is also a great vitamin A boost.

ingredients

¾ cup frozen mango chunks

½ small carrot, peeled

½ lime, peeled

3 fresh mint leaves

2 teaspoons honey

¾ cup unsweetened almond milk

directions

1. Place all ingredients into the 16-ounce Nutri Ninja® Cup in the order listed.

2. BLEND until smooth.

NINJA
KNOW-HOW

IT IS ESTIMATED THAT THERE ARE OVER 600 VARIETIES OF MINT. MOST ARE EASY TO GROW. TRY GROWING YOUR OWN.

PREP TIME: 5 minutes   MAKES: 1 serving   CONTAINER: 16-ounce Nutri Ninja® Cup

ginger pear melon defense

Ginger is a natural anti-inflammatory and aids in digestion. Choose ripe pears for extra sweetness.

ingredients

½ cup ice

1 ripe pear, quartered, cored

½ cup cantaloupe chunks

¼ lemon, peeled, seeded

½-inch piece fresh ginger, peeled

directions

1. Place all ingredients into the 16-ounce Nutri Ninja® Cup in the order listed.

2. BLEND until smooth.

NINJA
KNOW-HOW

ADD 1 TABLESPOON SPANISH BEE POLLEN FOR A SUPER FOOD BOOST.

PREP TIME: 5 minutes   MAKES: 1 serving   CONTAINER: 16-ounce Nutri Ninja® Cup

icy red purifier

Only 94 calories per serving, this is the perfect anytime drink.

ingredients

½ cup ice

1 cup fresh watermelon chunks

¾ cup raspberries

¼ cup water

directions

1. Place all ingredients into the 16-ounce Nutri Ninja® Cup in the order listed.

2. BLEND until smooth.

berries galore

A fiber and antioxidant-rich "berry delicious" nutrient extraction.

ingredients

¼ cup ice

½ cup blackberries

¼ cup raspberries

¼ cup blueberries

1 orange, peeled, quartered

directions

1. Place all ingredients into the 16-ounce Nutri Ninja® Cup in the order listed.

2. BLEND until smooth.

PREP TIME: 5 minutes   MAKES: 1 serving   CONTAINER: 16-ounce Nutri Ninja® Cup

mango melon mint fusion

With only 110 calories, this is the perfect vitamin C–packed refresher.

ingredients

¾ cup ice

½ cup honeydew melon chunks

½ cup fresh mango chunks

½ cup cantaloupe chunks chunks

3 fresh mint leaves

½ cup water

directions

1. Place all ingredients into the 16-ounce Nutri Ninja® Cup in the order listed.

2. BLEND until smooth.

 NINJA KNOW-HOW ADD 1 TABLESPOON SPANISH BEE POLLEN FOR A SUPER FOOD BOOST.

strawberry melon energy blast

Perfect 50-calorie refresher packed with your vitamin C for the day!

ingredients

¼ cup ice

¼ medium cucumber, peeled, halved

4 hulled strawberries

¾ cup cantaloupe chunks

directions

1. Place all ingredients into the 16-ounce Nutri Ninja® Cup in the order listed.

2. BLEND until smooth.

PREP TIME: 5 minutes   MAKES: 1 serving   CONTAINER: 16-ounce Nutri Ninja® Cup

yes, sprouts

Sprouts are a great way to get lots of extra micronutrients into your diet.

ingredients

½ cup ice

¾ cup water

½ ripe avocado, pitted, peeled

¼ cup loosely packed baby spinach

½ celery stalk, halved

½ lime, peeled

¼ cup of your favorite sprouts

directions

1. Place all ingredients into the 16-ounce Nutri Ninja® Cup in the order listed.

2. BLEND until smooth.

 TRY SPROUTING YOUR OWN SEEDS. IT'S EASY: JUST RINSE AND SOAK, THEN RINSE AND DRAIN ABOUT EVERY 8 HOURS FOR 3 DAYS.

KNOW-HOW

infused teas & waters

two berry tea

Try this calming tea filled with berry-rich antioxidants!

ingredients

½ cup ice

¾ cup chilled, strongly brewed, rooibos tea

¼ small ripe banana

1 tablespoon goji berries

½ cup fresh blueberries

directions

1. Place all ingredients into the 16-ounce Nutri Ninja® Cup in the order listed.

2. BLEND until smooth.

peach hydration

This is a great after-workout refresher.

ingredients

⅓ cup frozen peaches

½ lemon, seeded

1½ cups coconut water

directions

1. Place all ingredients into the 16-ounce Nutri Ninja® Cup in the order listed.

2. BLEND until smooth.

PREP TIME: 5 minutes   MAKES: 1 serving   CONTAINER: 16-ounce Nutri Ninja® Cup

INFUSED TEAS & WATERS

cherry lime rickey-ade

An all-natural energy-ade perfect after a good workout!

ingredients

½ cup frozen cherries

1 tablespoon fresh lime juice

1 cup coconut water

directions

1. Place all ingredients into the 16-ounce Nutri Ninja® Cup in the order listed.

2. BLEND until smooth.

3. Pour mixture through a fine mesh strainer to extract the flavored water.

NINJA KNOW-HOW STIR IN 1 TABLESPOON CHIA SEEDS, AFTER STRAINING, FOR YOUR VERY OWN HOMEMADE CHIA FRESCA.

PREP TIME: 5 minutes   **MAKES:** 1 serving   **CONTAINER:** 16-ounce Nutri Ninja® Cup

cucumber quencher

A refreshing, low-calorie pick-me-up.

ingredients

½ cup ice

⅛ teaspoon sea salt

⅓ English cucumber, quartered

3 fresh mint leaves

1¼ cups water

directions

1. Place all ingredients into the 16-ounce Nutri Ninja® Cup in the order listed.

2. BLEND until smooth.

pineapple mint water

Mint is a proven stomach soother and is great for your breath, too.

ingredients

¼ cup fresh pineapple chunks

3 fresh mint leaves

1½ cups cold water

directions

1. Place all ingredients into the 16-ounce Nutri Ninja® Cup in the order listed.

2. BLEND until smooth.

PREP TIME: 5 minutes   MAKES: 1 serving   CONTAINER: 16-ounce Nutri Ninja® Cup

almond chai tea

··

Used for thousands of years to promote general good health and well-being, Almond Chai Tea is rich in antioxidants and spices.

ingredients

3 pitted dates

2 tablespoons raw almonds

¼ small ripe banana

1¼ cups chilled, strongly brewed chai tea

directions

1. Place all ingredients into the 16-ounce Nutri Ninja® Cup in the order listed.

2. BLEND until smooth.

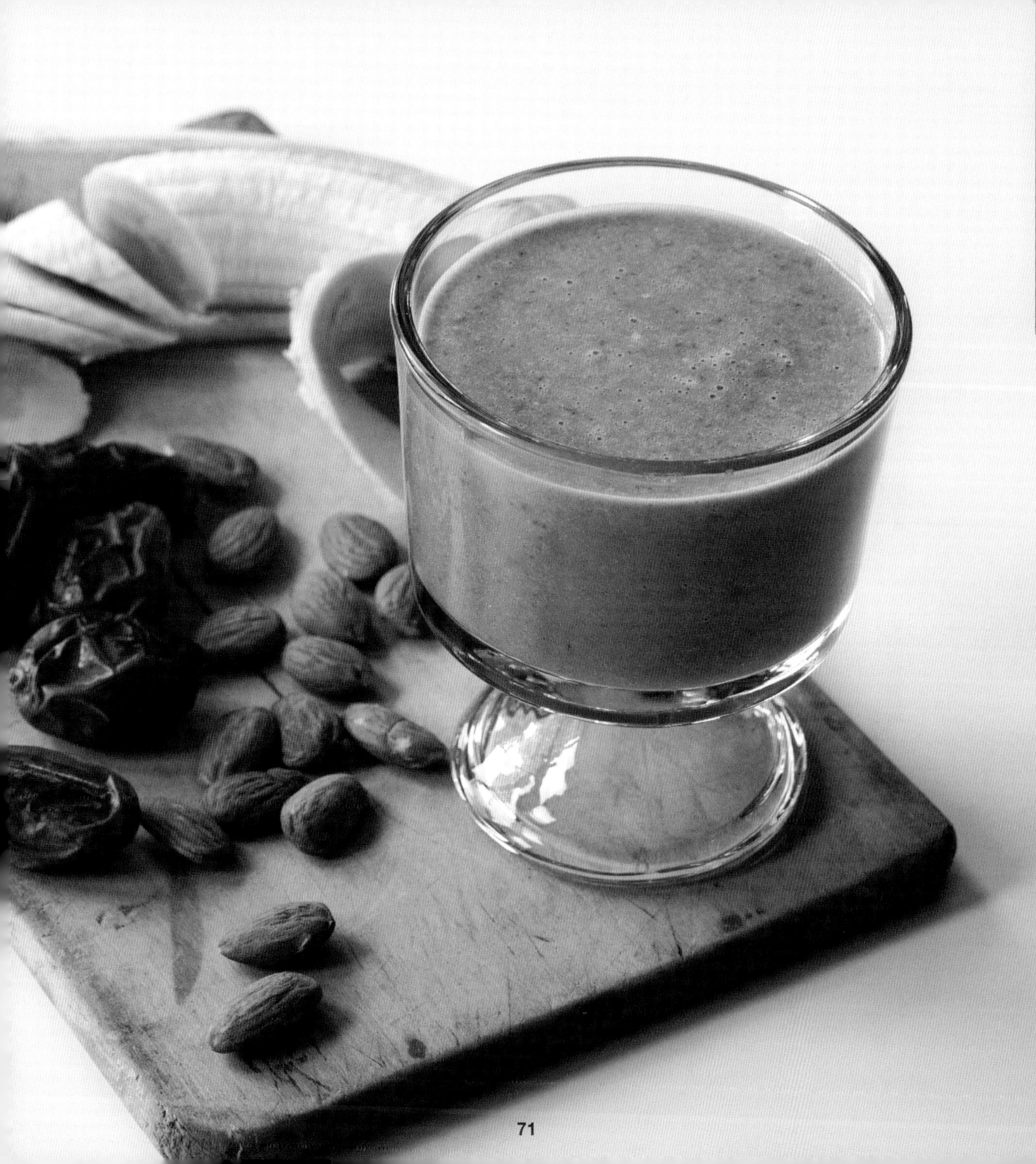

PREP TIME: 5 minutes   MAKES: 1 serving   CONTAINER: 16-ounce Nutri Ninja® Cup

chai spiced eye opener

The ginger and chai combine to a winter warming green super juice that will excite your taste buds!

ingredients

½ cup loosely packed baby spinach

½ ripe pear, quartered, cored

½ cup chilled, brewed chai tea (from tea bag)

¼ cup frozen mango chunks

⅛-inch piece fresh ginger, peeled

1 teaspoon fresh lemon juice

Dash sea salt

directions

1. Place all ingredients into the 16-ounce Nutri Ninja® Cup in the order listed.

2. BLEND until smooth.

melon fresca

This is a refreshing low-calorie drink, perfect for an afternoon snack.

ingredients

¼ cup ice

¼ cup cantaloupe chunks

¼ cup watermelon chunks

1½ cups water

⅛ teaspoon sea salt

directions

1. Place all ingredients into the 16-ounce Nutri Ninja® Cup in the order listed.

2. BLEND until smooth.

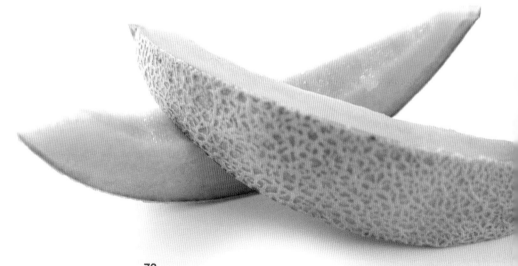

PREP TIME: 5 minutes   MAKES: 1 serving   CONTAINER: 16-ounce Nutri Ninja® Cup

coconut mango energyade

Create your own natural sports drink for active adults and children. High in potassium and perfect for hydration!

ingredients

¼ cup ripe mango chunks

1½ cups coconut water

6 fresh mint leaves

directions

1. Place all ingredients into the 16-ounce Nutri Ninja® Cup in the order listed.

2. BLEND until smooth.

PREP TIME: 5 minutes MAKES: 1 serving CONTAINER: 16-ounce Nutri Ninja® Cup

pear energy

Take on pure pear energy along with the green goodness of spinach.

ingredients

½ pear, cut in half, cored

½ cup spinach

½ lemon, peeled, seeded

2 teaspoons honey

1 cup cold, brewed green tea

¾ cup ice

directions

1. Place all ingredients into the 16-ounce Nutri Ninja® Cup in the order listed.
2. BLEND until smooth.

PREP TIME: 10 minutes   COOK TIME: 10–15 minutes   MAKES: 8 servings   CONTAINER: 40-ounce Processor Bowl

chicken apple sausage patties

Making sausage is a snap in your Ninja®.

ingredients

1 small onion, peeled, quartered

2 apples, peeled, cored, quartered

⅓ cup fresh sage leaves

1 tablespoon olive oil

1 lb. uncooked boneless, skinless chicken thighs, cut in 2-inch cubes

pinch of cinnamon

¾ teaspoon kosher salt

¾ teaspoon fresh ground pepper

directions

1. Preheat oven to 350°F. Line a baking sheet with parchment paper; set aside. Place the onion, apples, and sage into the 40-ounce Processor Bowl. PULSE, using short pulses, until finely chopped, about 5 or times.

2. Heat the olive oil in a medium skillet over medium heat. Add the onion, the apple mixture and saute 3 to 5 minutes, until soft. Remove from heat and place in a large bowl.

3. Place the cubed chicken into the 40-ounce Processor Bowl. PULSE, using long pulses, until finely ground, 6 to 8 times. Add the ground chicken to the bowl with the onion and apple mixture. Add the cinnamon and season with salt and pepper. Mix well, using your hands.

4. Form mixture into 8 patties and bake on a parchment line cookie sheet for about 10 to 12 minutes, or until fully cooked.

NINJA KNOW-HOW USE CHICKEN OR TURKEY BREAST FOR A LIGHTER OPTION.

PREP TIME: 15 minutes   COOK TIME: 20 minutes   MAKES: 4 servings   CONTAINER: 40-ounce Processor Bowl

turkey hash

A wonderfully delicious and healthier way to make hash.

ingredients

½ medium onion, quartered

½ red bell pepper, seeded, quartered

1 clove garlic

1 lb. uncooked turkey breast, cut in 2-inch cubes

1 tablespoon vegetable oil

1 lb. cooked sweet potato, peeled, chopped

¾ cup low-sodium chicken broth

1 teaspoon dried thyme

¾ teaspoon kosher salt

½ teaspoon ground black pepper

¼ cup chopped green onion

directions

1. Place the onion, red pepper, and garlic into the 40-ounce Processor Bowl and PULSE, using short pulses, to desired chop. Remove vegetables and set aside.

2. Place the cubed turkey into the 40-ounce Processor Bowl and PULSE, using long pulses, until finely ground.

3. Heat the oil in a medium skillet over medium heat. Add vegetable mixture. Saute 3 to 5 minutes, until soft.

4. Add the ground turkey and cook for 4 minutes, then add the cooked sweet potatoes, chicken broth, thyme, salt, black pepper, and green onion then cook for 10 minutes or until turkey is cooked through, stirring occasionally.

NINJA KNOW-HOW WITH SCRAMBLED EGG WHITES FOR A COMPLETE BREAKFAST.

BREAKFASTS

tomato basil scramble

· ·

This recipe is an easy and simple way to make fluffy eggs and veggies in the morning!

ingredients

4 large eggs

¼ vine-ripe tomato

¼ cup shredded mozzarella

¼ cup fresh basil leaves

⅛ teaspoon kosher salt

⅛ teaspoon ground black pepper

2 teaspoons unsalted butter

directions

1. Place the eggs, tomato, mozzarella, basil, salt, and black pepper into the 16-ounce Chopper and PULSE to finely chop, using short pulses.

2. Heat the butter in a nonstick skillet and place over medium high heat. Add the egg mixture, then cook, stirring frequently until fluffy and cooked through.

 NINJA KNOW-HOW FOR A LIGHTER BREAKFAST, SUBSTITUTE 4 LARGE EGGS WITH 6 EGG WHITES. ALSO, USE COOKING SPRAY INSTEAD OF THE BUTTER.

PREP TIME: 10 minutes   COOK TIME: 15 minutes   MAKES: 2 servings   CONTAINER: 40-ounce Processor Bowl

turkey sausage burrito

This is just spicy enough to give it a south-of-the-border zing.

ingredients

½ medium onion, halved

½ green bell pepper, seeded, halved

1 teaspoon chipotle in adobo sauce

¾ cup crushed tomato

1 clove garlic

1 tablespoon chili powder

2 teaspoons ground cumin

1 teaspoon dried oregano

½ cup low-sodium chicken broth

¼ teaspoon kosher salt

2 7-inch whole wheat flour tortillas, heated through

1½ cups crumbled turkey breakfast sausage, warmed

4 large eggs, scrambled

½ cup shredded low-fat Colby Jack cheese

directions

1. Place the onion, bell pepper, chipotle, crushed tomato, garlic, chili powder, cumin, oregano, chicken broth, and salt into the 40-ounce Processor Bowl and BLEND until smooth. Place mixture in a medium saucepan, bring to a boil, then reduce to a simmer for 10 minutes.

2. Lay the tortillas on the work surface and top with cooked turkey sausage, scrambled eggs, and cheese. Roll to close.

3. To serve, place burrito on a plate and top with warm sauce.

NINJA KNOW-HOW YOU CAN SUBSTITUTE CHICKEN SAUSAGE FOR THE TURKEY.

coconut lime bars

Coconut and fresh lime zest combine for a tropical twist to these easy-to-make snack bars.

ingredients

1 cup dried apricots

2 cups toasted macadamia nuts

½ cup unsweetened, shredded coconut

2 tablespoons hemp seeds

1 teaspoon fresh lime zest

1 teaspoon fresh lime juice

1 tablespoon agave syrup

1 tablespoon water

⅛ teaspoon sea salt

¼ cup pumpkin seeds

directions

1. Line an 8x8-inch baking dish with plastic wrap; set aside. Place the dried apricots into the 40-ounce Pitcher and PULSE 5 times, using long pulses.

2. Add the remaining ingredients, except for the pumpkin seeds, and PULSE 10 to 15 more times, using long pulses.

3. Add the pumpkin seeds and PULSE 2 times, using short pulses. Spread mixture into the prepared baking dish and press down to evenly disperse. Allow to chill for at least 2 hours before cutting into 16 equal pieces. Store in the refrigerator, covered, up to 1 week.

PREP TIME: 20 minutes   COOK TIME: 10 minutes   MAKES: 4 servings   CONTAINER: 40-ounce Processor Bowl

zucchini quinoa latkes

A lighter delicious twist to traditional potato pancakes with added protein from the quinoa.

ingredients

3 cups chopped zucchini

2 large eggs

½ teaspoon kosher salt

½ teaspoon ground black pepper

¼ cup matzo meal

½ cup cooked quinoa

Olive oil for sautéing

½ cup sour cream

2 tablespoons chives

directions

1. Place the zucchini, eggs, salt, and black pepper into the 40-ounce Processor Bowl and PULSE, using short pulses, to finely chop.

2. Place mixture into a large bowl, then add the matzo meal and cooked quinoa, stirring to combine.

3. Heat 1 tablespoon of olive oil in a nonstick skillet over medium heat. Drop a spoonful of the batter into oil and press lightly to flatten. Cook for 2 minutes per side or until golden brown. Repeat until all batter is gone.

4. To serve, top each latke with sour cream and chives.

PREP TIME: 15 minutes + 30 minutes rest   COOK TIME: 45 minutes   MAKES: 8 servings   CONTAINER: 40-ounce Processor Bowl

chorizo & pepper egg bake

This is a high-energy breakfast with a little bit of wake-me-up kick.

ingredients

6 large eggs

2 cups low-fat milk

¼ teaspoon kosher salt

¼ teaspoon ground black pepper

1 tablespoon vegetable oil

1 lb. cooked chorizo, chopped

1 poblano pepper, seeded, chopped

½ medium onion, chopped

½ lb. whole wheat bread, cut in ½-inch strips

1 cup shredded cheddar cheese

2 tablespoons chopped fresh cilantro

1 ripe avocado, pitted, peeled, sliced

directions

1. Lightly spray a 9x9-inch baking dish with vegetable cooking spray; set aside.

2. Place the eggs, milk, salt, and black pepper into the 40-ounce Processor Bowl. Blend until smooth.

3. Heat oil in a medium skillet over medium heat. Add the chorizo and saute about 5 minutes, until browned.

4. Add the pepper and onion and cook for 6 minutes.

5. Arrange half the bread slices in the prepared baking dish. Pour half of the egg mixture on top. Add half the chorizo and pepper mixture, spread evenly, then top with cheese, pressing to submerge ingredients. Repeat layering the bread, egg, and chorizo mixture, and cheese. Let strata stand for 30 minutes at room temperature before baking.

6. Preheat oven to 350°F. Bake uncovered for 40 minutes or until a knife inserted into the center comes out clean. Remove from oven and let stand for 5 minutes, then top with cilantro and avocado.

PREP TIME: 15 minutes + 30 minutes rest   COOK TIME: 35 minutes   MAKES: 8 servings   CONTAINER: 40-ounce Processor Bowl

monte cristo casserole

If you love a Monte Cristo sandwich, you will love this casserole.

ingredients

8 ounces cubed low-sodium deli turkey

8 ounces cubed 98% fat-free deli ham

8 ounces cubed Swiss cheese, chunked

6 large eggs

2 cups low-fat milk

½ loaf French bread, cubed

¾ cup low-sugar strawberry preserves

directions

1. Lightly spray a loaf pan with vegetable cooking spray; set aside.

2. Place the turkey, ham, and cheese into the 40-ounce Processor Bowl. PULSE, using short pulses, until finely chopped. Remove ingredients and set aside.

3. Place the eggs and milk into the 40-ounce Processor Bowl and BLEND until smooth.

4. Place the egg mixture into a mixing bowl and add the bread. Stir to coat and let sit for 30 minutes to absorb the egg mixture.

5. Arrange half the bread mixture in the prepared baking dish. Top with the turkey mixture and dollop the preserves throughout. Place remaining bread mixture on top, pressing to submerge ingredients.

6. Preheat oven to 350°F. Bake uncovered for 35 minutes or until a knife inserted into the center comes out clean.

NINJA KNOW-HOW | SUBSTITUTE WHOLE GRAIN BREAD FOR FRENCH BREAD FOR ADDED FIBER.

PREP TIME: 15 minutes + 30 minutes rest   PREP TIME: 25 minutes   MAKES: 8 servings   CONTAINER: 40-ounce Processor Bowl

spinach & feta strata

This recipe is wonderfully delicious. Great for a morning family brunch.

ingredients

5 large eggs

1 cup half & half

½ cup cubed Monterey Jack cheese

½ cup cubed feta cheese

¼ teaspoon ground nutmeg

½ teaspoon salt

¼ teaspoon black pepper

1 cup cooked spinach, well drained (about 6 cups fresh)

1 loaf day-old French bread, crusts removed, torn into bite-sized pieces

directions

1. Lightly spray a 9-inch round baking pan with vegetable cooking spray; set aside.

2. Add the eggs, half & half, cheeses, nutmeg, salt and pepper to 40-ounce Processor Bowl. BLEND until smooth. Add the spinach and PULSE, using short short pulses, 2 to 3 times.

3. Coat a round 9-inch baking pan with cooking spray. Place the bread into the pan and pour the spinach and egg mixture over the bread. Place into the fridge for 30 minutes to allow the egg mixture to soak into the bread.

4. Preheat oven to 350°F. Bake for 20 to 25 minutes, until puffed and golden brown. Serve hot.

NINJA KNOW-HOW | YOU CAN SUBSTITUTE ANY DAY-OLD BREAD.

fresh veggie frittata

Perfect brunch fare!

ingredients

1 stalk broccoli, cut in 2-inch florets

½ red bell pepper, seeded, quartered

¼ onion

1 clove garlic

1 tablespoon olive oil

6 eggs

¾ cup grated Parmesan cheese, divided

½ teaspoon dried basil

½ teaspoon kosher salt

⅛ teaspoon ground black pepper

directions

1. Preheat oven to 350°F. Spray a 9 x 9-inch square baking dish with vegetable cooking spray; set aside.

2. Place the broccoli, red pepper, onion, and garlic into the 40-ounce Processor Bowl. PULSE, using short pulses, until roughly chopped.

3. Heat the olive oil in a medium skillet over medium-high heat. Add chopped vegetables and sauté about 10 minutes, until soft. Transfer to prepared baking dish.

4. Add the eggs, ½ cup parmesan, basil, salt and pepper to the 40-ounce Processor Bowl. Blend for 15 to 20 seconds, until smooth.

5. Pour egg mixture over vegetables and sprinkle remaining cheese on top. Bake 20 to 22 minutes or until center is set and top is lightly browned.

buckwheat boost pancakes

Wholesome low-fat pancakes are great on their own or topped with some fresh fruit.

ingredients

1 cup buckwheat flour

1 cup all-purpose flour

2½ teaspoons baking powder

2 teaspoons sugar

1 teaspoon salt

2 eggs

⅓ cup tablespoons vegetable oil

¼ cup honey

1½ cups skim milk

directions

1. Place the buckwheat flour, all-purpose flour, baking powder, sugar, salt, eggs, oil, honey, and milk into the 40-ounce Processor Bowl and BLEND until smooth. Let batter set for 1 hour.

2. Lightly spray a nonstick skillet with vegetable cooking spray and place over medium heat. Flip and continue cooking until center is puffed and springs back when gently pushed.

NINJA
KNOW-HOW
FOR AN EVEN HEALTHIER VERSION, SUBSTITUTE WHOLE WHEAT FLOUR FOR THE ALL-PURPOSE FLOUR.

PREP TIME: 5 minutes   MAKES: 1 serving   CONTAINER: 16-ounce Nutri Ninja® Cup

autumn balancer

Beat the bloated blues with this slimming sipper.

ingredients

½ cup ice

½ cup cooked sweet potato

¾ cup unsweetened almond milk

1 tablespoon maple syrup

½ teaspoon flax seed

⅛ teaspoon ground turmeric

⅛ teaspoon kosher salt

directions

1. Place all ingredients into the 16-ounce Nutri Ninja® Cup in the order listed.

2. BLEND until smooth.

PREP TIME: 20 minutes MAKES: 2 serving CONTAINER: 40-ounce Processor Bowl

banana & oats

You will love this portable oatmeal breakfast loaded with micronutrient-rich walnuts and fruit.

ingredients

2 small bananas

1 cup cold cooked oatmeal

2 tablespoons shelled walnuts

2 tablespoons maple syrup

½ teaspoon ground cinnamon

1¾ cups nonfat milk

1¼ cups nonfat plain yogurt

directions

1. Place all ingredients into the 40-ounce Processor Bowl in the order listed.

2. BLEND until smooth.

NINJA
KNOW-HOW

MAKE SURE YOUR YOGURT CONTAINS ACTIVE CULTURES. MOST BRANDS WILL HAVE A GRAPHIC THAT SAYS "LIVE AND ACTIVE CULTURES" AND WILL LIST THE SPECIFIC CULTURES.

PREP TIME: 5 minutes   MAKES: 1 serving   CONTAINER: 16-ounce Nutri Ninja® Cup

chocolate cherry protein blast

This is a perfect meal replacement shake, packed with 10 grams of fiber and 17 grams of protein.

ingredients

½ ripe avocado, pitted, peeled

1 cup unsweetened almond milk

1 teaspoon unsweetened cocoa powder

1 scoop chocolate protein powder

¾ cup frozen cherries

directions

1. Place all ingredients into the 16-ounce Nutri Ninja® Cup in the order listed.

2. BLEND until smooth.

the sunflower

Sunflower butter delivers omega-3 fats and proteins, making this a satisfying on-the-go breakfast or snack.

ingredients

½ small ripe banana, halved

¾ cup unsweetened vanilla almond milk

2 tablespoons sunflower butter

⅛ teaspoon ground cinnamon

2 teaspoons pure maple syrup

½ cup ice

directions

1. Place all ingredients into the 16-ounce Nutri Ninja® Cup in the order listed.

2. BLEND until smooth.

trail mix in a glass

Great for those with an active lifestyle. All the flavors of a trail mix whipped up in a nourishing breakfast.

ingredients

½ cup ice

2 tablespoons raw unsalted almonds

2 tablespoons raw unsalted pumpkin seeds

2 teaspoons raw sesame seeds

2 tablespoons goji berries

2 tablespoons pomegranate juice

¾ cup unsweetened vanilla almond milk

2 tablespoons honey

directions

1. Place all ingredients into the 16-ounce Nutri Ninja® Cup in the order listed.

2. BLEND until smooth.

PREP TIME: 5 minutes   MAKES: 1 serving   CONTAINER: 16-ounce Nutri Ninja® Cup

top o' the mornin'

A perfect on-the-go breakfast filled with protein, potassium, and vitamin C!

ingredients

½ cup ice

1 seedless orange, peeled, quartered

1 cup unsweetened almond milk

1 scoop whey protein powder

½ teaspoon ground cinnamon

1 small banana, quartered

directions

1. Place all ingredients into the 16-ounce Nutri Ninja® Cup in the order listed.

2. BLEND until smooth.

apple almond power smoothie

Almond milk is lactose-free. Almond butter is a great source of vitamin E and contains a nutritional punch. A great protein-filled pick-me-up after a workout or long walk.

ingredients

½ cup ice

1 green apple, peeled, quartered

1 tablespoon almond butter

1 scoop whey vanilla protein powder

1 cup unsweetened almond milk

1 small banana, peeled, halved

directions

1. Place all ingredients into the 16-ounce Nutri Ninja® Cup in the order listed.

2. BLEND until smooth.

PREP TIME: 7 minutes MAKES: 1 serving CONTAINER: 16-ounce Nutri Ninja® Cup

coffee soymoothie

This creamy coffee drink has both almond butter and silken tofu to get you started in the morning!

ingredients

½ cup ice

1 tablespoon agave nectar

⅛ teaspoon cardamom powder

½ tablespoon almond butter

⅓ cup silken tofu

½ cup chilled, strongly brewed decaf coffee

directions

1. Place all ingredients into the 16-ounce Nutri Ninja® Cup in the order listed.
2. BLEND until smooth.

PREP TIME: 5 minutes   MAKES: 1 serving   CONTAINER: 16-ounce Nutri Ninja® Cup

bright side mocha shake

A high-energy, early morning "get me up" beverage.

ingredients

1 cup ice

½ small ripe banana

¼ cup chilled brewed coffee

1½ tablespoons almond butter

1 teaspoon unsweetened cocoa powder

1 teaspoon agave nectar

½ cup unsweetened almond milk

Dash sea salt

directions

1. Place all ingredients into the 16-ounce Nutri Ninja® Cup in the order listed.

2. BLEND until smooth.

PREP TIME: 25 minutes   COOK TIME: 30 seconds   MAKES: 2 cups   CONTAINER: 40-ounce Processor Bowl

kale & sunflower pesto

A new twist on an old favorite! A great way to use up those extra greens—spinach works well, too!

ingredients

½ medium bunch kale, stems removed

¼ cup packed fresh basil leaves

1 large clove garlic

¼ cup roasted, unsalted sunflower seeds

2 tablespoons grated parmesan

zest and juice of ½ lemon

Sea salt to taste

⅛ teaspoon ground black pepper

¼ cup olive oil, plus more as needed

directions

1. Bring 4 quarts of salted water to a boil. Blanch the kale leaves for 30 seconds and upon removal, immediately plunge into ice water. Squeeze the kale leaves dry and set aside.

2. Add the kale, basil, garlic, sunflower seeds, Parmesan cheese, lemon juice/zest, olive oil, and a pinch of salt and pepper to the 40-ounce Processor Bowl.

3. PULSE 5 times, using long pulses, and then BLEND continuously until desired consistency is achieved. Add more oil if needed.

NINJA KNOW-HOW TOAST YOUR OWN SUNFLOWER SEEDS. TOSS SEEDS GENTLY IN A DRY SKILLET, OVER MEDIUM HEAT, UNTIL GOLDEN BROWN.

PREP TIME: 10 minutes   MAKES: 1½ cups   CONTAINER: 16-ounce Chopper

mango rum remoulade

Cornichons are small pickled gherkins, a variety of cucumber that add tang to this tasty remoulade. This recipe is perfect as a sauce for seafood or poultry.

ingredients

¾ cup light mayonnaise

¼ cup cornichons

1 tablespoon capers

1½ tablespoons dark rum

½ ripe mango, peeled, pitted, cut in 2-inch chunks

1 tablespoons water

¼ teaspoon kosher salt

¼ teaspoon ground black pepper

directions

1. Place all ingredients into the 16-ounce Chopper in the order listed.

2. PULSE 5 to 7 times, using short pulses.

NINJA KNOW-HOW — SERVE WITH FISH OR PORK SANDWICHES OR CHICKEN CUTLETS.

pineapple cilantro dipping sauce

Of all the bright green herbs out there, cilantro—the fresh, leafy stalks of the coriander plant—are loved by the millions who pile it on soups, salsas, wraps, and roll-ups.

ingredients

1 cups fresh pineapple chunks

½ small serrano chili, seeded

¼ small white onion, quartered

¼ cup fresh cilantro leaves

1½ tablespoons freshly squeezed
lime juice

1 tablespoon coconut oil

Kosher salt and pepper to taste

directions

1. Place all ingredients into the 16-ounce Chopper in the order listed.

2. PULSE until desired consistency, using short pulses.

NINJA **KNOW-HOW** — WRAP CILANTRO IN A WET PAPER TOWEL AND STORE IN THE CRISPER DRAWER TO KEEP FRESH AND CRISP.

PREP TIME: 10 minutes   COOK TIME: 25 minutes   MAKES: 1¾ cups   CONTAINER: 16-ounce Chopper

fresh & healthy ketchup relish

The Ninja® makes it easy to make your own homemade ketchup relish with only 5 calories per serving.

ingredients

¾ cup yellow onion, quartered

½ red bell pepper, seeded, chopped

1 clove garlic

2 vine-ripe tomatoes, quartered, seeded

1 tablespoon, plus 2 teaspoons apple cider vinegar

½ teaspoon molasses

¼ teaspoon ground black pepper

¾ cup kosher baby dill pickles, halved

1 tablespoon Dijon mustard

directions

1. Place 1/2 cup onion, red bell pepper, garlic, tomato, vinegar, molasses, and ground black pepper into the 16-ounce Chopper. PULSE until finely chopped, using short pulses.

2. Pour the tomato mixture into a medium saucepan and cook over medium-low heat for 25 minutes, stirring occasionally.

3. Remove from the heat and chill for 1 hour.

4. Place the remaining 1/4 cup onion, pickles, Dijon mustard, and the cooled tomato mixture into the 16-ounce Chopper. PULSE until finely chopped, using long pulses.

NINJA
KNOW-HOW

IN A COVERED CONTAINER, CHILL THE RELISH OVERNIGHT IN THE REFRIGERATOR TO HELP DEVELOP AND MARRY THE FLAVORS.

PREP TIME: 30 minutes   COOK TIME: 30 minutes   MAKES: 1 serving   CONTAINER: 40-ounce Processor Bowl

sundried tomato sauce

Why buy the sugar-laden store bought type when you can make your own? Add roasted peppers, mushrooms, or roasted garlic for your own personalized flavors.

ingredients

¼ onion

2 cloves garlic

1 tablespoon olive oil

1 (14.5 ounce) can whole tomatoes and juice

¼ cup sun-dried tomatoes packed in olive oil

¼ cup dry red wine

¼ teaspoon red pepper flakes

¼ cup basil, chopped

kosher salt and pepper to taste

directions

1. Place all ingredients into the 40-ounce Pitcher in the order listed.

2. PULSE 3 to 5 times, using long pulses, until desired consistency.

3. Pour sauce into a medium saucepan and simmer 20 to 25 minutes.

NINJA KNOW-HOW YOU CAN SUBSTITUTE 8 RIPE ROMA TOMATOES, JUST SIMMER FOR TWO HOURS INSTEAD.

PREP TIME: 15 minutes   COOK TIME: 15 minutes   MAKES: 2 cups   CONTAINER: 16-ounce Chopper

tandoori marinade

This delicious tandoori marinade, perfect for lamb, is also a great complement to grilled meats and seafood.

ingredients

2 ounces dried ancho chili peppers

1 teaspoon fresh ginger

2 cloves garlic, peeled

½ cup fresh cilantro leaves

2 tablespoons garam masala powder

⅛ teaspoon ground nutmeg

1 tablespoon freshly squeezed lemon juice

1 cup nonfat Greek yogurt

½ cup cold water

directions

1. Place the dried ancho chili peppers into a small saucepot and pour just enough water to cover the peppers. Bring to a boil, reduce to a simmer, and cook for 10 minutes. Strain peppers and then cool. Remove the top and seeds from the peppers.

2. Place all ingredients into the 16-ounce Chopper. PULSE until desired consistency, using short pulses.

 NINJA KNOW-HOW COOK THE SPICES FOR ADDED FLAVOR OR SIMPLY MIX AND USE.

113

PREP TIME: 10 minutes   MAKES: 1cup   CONTAINER: 16-ounce Chopper

cilantro mayonnaise

Make your own homemade mayonnaise, with the addition of flavorful cilantro, for a different take.

ingredients

¾ cup packed, fresh cilantro leaves

3 egg yolks

1 teaspoon Dijon mustard

1 teaspoon lemon juice

½ teaspoon kosher salt

2 teaspoons cold water

¾ cup olive oil

directions

1. Place all ingredients into the 16-ounce Chopper in the order listed.

2. PULSE until desired consistency, using short pulses.

 NINJA KNOW-HOW SERVE WITH A TURKEY BURGER, CHICKEN PANINI, OR EVEN BRUSHED ON A PIECE OF FISH.

passion fruit vinaigrette

Try this dressing served over greens, fruit, or even a chicken breast.

ingredients

½ cup frozen passion fruit pulp, thawed

2 tablespoons Dijon mustard

¼ cup rice wine vinegar

3 tablespoons honey

2 tablespoons fresh thyme leaves

½ teaspoon kosher salt

3 tablespoons extra-virgin olive oil

¾ cup fat-free sour cream

directions

1. Place all ingredients into the 16-ounce Nutri Ninja® Cup in the order listed.

2. BLEND until smooth.

NINJA KNOW-HOW YOU CAN SUBSTITUTE MAPLE SYRUP FOR THE HONEY.

PREP TIME: 15 minutes CHILL TIME: 1 hour   MAKES: 2 cups CONTAINER: 16-ounce Chopper

country herb dressing

Sprouts are a great way to get lots of extra micronutrients into your diet.

ingredients

½ cup buttermilk

1 cup mayonnaise

1 tablespoon lemon juice

¼ cup loosely packed fresh parsley leaves

12 sprigs fresh chive, cut in thirds

⅛ cup fresh tarragon leaves

1 clove garlic

1 teaspoon ground black pepper

½ teaspoon kosher salt

directions

1. Place all ingredients into the 16-ounce Chopper in the order listed.

2. PULSE until desired consistency, using short pulses.

PREP TIME: 20 minutes   COOK TIME: 25 minutes   MAKES: 4 servings   CONTAINER: 40-ounce Processor Bowl

vegetable enchilada soup

Plantains are the fruit of the Musa paradisiaca, a type of banana plant.

ingredients

½ medium yellow onion, halved

1 small zucchini, quartered

1 can (10 ounces) mild enchilada sauce

2 tablespoons mild green chilies

1 tablespoon chili powder

1 teaspoon ground cumin

2 teaspoons dried oregano

1 cup loosely packed fresh cilantro leaves

2 tablespoons vegetable oil

4 cups vegetable broth

¾ cup fresh corn kernels

½ cup plantains, cooked, 1-inch slices

1 can (15.5 ounces) pinto beans, drained

½ teaspoon kosher salt

½ teaspoon ground black pepper

¼ cup sliced black olives

⅓ cup shredded Mexican blend cheese

directions

1. Place the onion and zucchini into the 40-ounce Processor Bowl and PULSE, using short pulses, until finely chopped. Remove mixture and set aside.

2. In the same Processor Bowl, place the enchilada sauce, chilies, chili powder, cumin, oregano, and cilantro. BLEND until smooth.

3. Heat oil in a large saucepan over medium heat. Add the onion and zucchini mixture and saute 5 to 10 minutes, until soft.

4. Add the puréed mixture, vegetable broth, corn, plantains, pinto beans, salt, and black pepper to the saucepan and bring to a boil. Reduce heat and simmer for 15 minutes, stirring occasionally.

5. To serve, ladle soup in a bowl and garnish each serving with black olives and cheese.

lentil & ham soup

Compared with other types of dried beans, lentils are relatively quick and easy to prepare. They readily absorb a variety of wonderful flavors from other foods.

ingredients

½ **medium yellow onion, halved**

1 **carrot, peeled, quartered**

1 **celery stalk, quartered**

1 **clove garlic**

1 **8-ounce ham steak, cubed**

2 **tablespoons vegetable oil**

5 **cups low-sodium chicken broth**

1 **cup crushed tomatoes**

¾ **teaspoon dried oregano**

¾ **teaspoon dried basil**

½ **teaspoon kosher salt**

½ **teaspoon ground black pepper**

1 **cup dried lentils, picked through for stones**

directions

1. Place the onion, carrot, celery and garlic into the 40-ounce Processor Bowl and PULSE, using short pulses, until finely chopped. Remove, set aside and repeat with ham, until finely chopped.

2. Heat oil in a large saucepan over medium heat. Add ham and vegetables and saute for 5 minutes, stirring occasionally.

3. Add the chicken broth, tomatoes, oregano, basil, salt, black pepper, and lentils and bring to a boil. Reduce heat and simmer for 20 minutes, or until lentils are tender, stirring occasionally.

butternut squash soup with chicken sausage

This soup is full of root vegetables, with lean protein from the chicken apple sausage.

ingredients

3 tablespoons olive oil

1 large yellow onion, chopped

1 cup raw cashews

1 large apple, peeled, cored, chopped

1 large carrot, peeled, chopped

2 lbs. butternut squash, cubed

1 teaspoon fresh thyme leaves

1 bay leaf

4 cups vegetable stock, plus more to thin if desired

½ teaspoon kosher salt, or more to taste

Black pepper, to taste

Chicken Apple Sausage Patties (see page 78), crumbled, warmed

directions

1. Place the onion, apple and carrots into the 40-ounce Processor Bowl in the order listed. PULSE, using short pulses, until finely chopped.

2. Heat oil in a large saucepan over medium heat. Add the chopped onion mixture and saute about 5 minutes, until soft.

3. Add the squash, thyme, and bay leaf and cook 5 minutes. Add the broth and stir to combine. Bring the soup to a boil and simmer 20 to 25 minutes, until squash if fork tender. Remove from heat and discard bay leaf. Allow soup to cool to room temperature.

4. Working in two batches, ladle half of the soup into the 40-ounce Processor Bowl. BLEND until smooth. Pour puréed soup into a large bowl. Repeat with remaining soup. Return all puréed soup to saucepan and simmer until heated through. Top with crumbled sausage and serve.

 NINJA KNOW-HOW   FOR A VEGAN VERSION, ADD CANNELINI BEANS INSTEAD OF THE SAUSAGE.

PREP TIME: 8 minutes   COOK TIME: 15–20 minutes   MAKES: 6 servings   CONTAINER: 40-ounce Processor Bowl

tomato basil soup

This soup is delicious as a sauce or soup, and filled with the antioxidant, lycopene.

ingredients

1 (28 ounce) can crushed tomatoes

2 tablespoons tomato paste

1 clove garlic

1 cup vegetable broth

½ cup loosely packed fresh basil

¼ teaspoon salt

½ teaspoon ground black pepper

directions

1. Place all ingredients into the 40-ounce Processor Bowl in the order listed.

2. PULSE until smooth, using long pulses.

3. Pour soup into a medium saucepan and simmer 15 to 20 minutes.

NINJA KNOW-HOW — TO MAKE THIS SOUP CREAMY WHILE KEEPING IT HEALTHIER, TRY ADDING ½ CUP FAT FAT-FREE HALF & HALF.

PREP TIME: 10 minutes   **MAKES:** 4 servings   **CONTAINER:** 16-ounce Chopper/40-ounce Processor Bowl

broccoli cheddar soup

Loaded with healthy broccoli, this hearty soup is cheesy, easy to make, and delicious!

ingredients

½ **yellow onion, cut in half**

1 **clove garlic**

½ **tablespoon canola oil**

3 **cups broccoli florets**

2 **cups low-sodium vegetable broth**

¼ **cup half & half**

½ **cup shredded cheddar cheese**

Kosher salt and ground black pepper to taste

directions

1. Place the onion and garlic into the 16-ounce Chopper. PULSE 3 to 5 times, using short pulses, until finely chopped.

2. Heat the oil in a medium saucepan over medium heat. Add the chopped onions and garlic and sweat for 5 minutes, until translucent.

3. Add the broccoli florets to the pot and cook 1 to 2 minutes. Add vegetable broth, bring to boil, reduce heat to low and cook 25 minutes until broccoli is fork tender. Add the half & half and the cheddar cheese, and remove from the heat. Allow to cool to room temperature.

4. Working in batches, place half of the cooled soup into the 40-ounce Processor Bowl and blend until smooth.

5. Place soup into a large bowl and repeat with remaining soup. Return puréed soup back to saucepan and simmer until heated through. Season with salt and pepper to taste. Season with salt and pepper to taste.

PREP TIME: 5 minutes   MAKES: 8 servings   CONTAINER: 40-ounce Processor Bowl

gazpacho

....

Gazpacho, a refreshing summertime soup, is packed full of flavor and nutrition!

ingredients

1 small red onion, quartered

2 English cucumbers, cut in 2-inch chunks

1 yellow pepper, quartered, seeded

1 red pepper, quartered, seeded

3 lbs. fresh tomatoes; peeled, seeded, and chopped

3½ teaspoons kosher salt

¼ cup red wine vinegar

¼ cup olive oil

48 ounces tomato juice

1 teaspoon garlic, minced

directions

1. Place each of the ingredients, starting with red onions, into the 40-ounce Processor Bowl, one ingredient at a time, and PULSE until finely chopped, using short pulses.

2. Combine all of the finely chopped vegetables into a large mixing bowl and season with salt, vinegar, olive oil, tomato juice, and garlic. Refrigerate overnight to allow flavors to meld or serve immediately.

PREP TIME: 5 minutes   MAKES: 4 servings   CONTAINER: 40-ounce Processor Bowl

loaded chicken salad

This salad is not only easy, but depending on how many pulses you give, you can chop to your liking – finely chopped or with larger chunks of chicken.

ingredients

1 celery stalk, quartered

2 cups cubed, cooked chicken breast

¼ cup shelled walnuts

⅓ cup mayonnaise

½ teaspoon kosher salt

¼ teaspoon ground black pepper

¼ teaspoon onion powder

⅓ cup red grapes

directions

1. Place all ingredients into the 40-ounce Processor Bowl in the order listed.

2. PULSE, using short pulses, until using short pulses, until finely chopped, about 5 to 7 times.

curried chicken salad

An exotic Indian spin to add some spice to a classic lunch favorite.

ingredients

2 cups cubed, cooked chicken breast

¼ cup loosely packed cilantro leaves

¼ small red onion

1 celery stalk, quartered

⅓ cup mayonnaise

2 teaspoons curry powder

2 teaspoons fresh lime juice

½ teaspoon kosher salt

⅛ teaspoon ground black pepper

directions

1. Place all ingredients into the 40-ounce Processor Bowl in the order listed.

2. PULSE, using short pulses, until finely chopped, about 5 to 7 times.

white bean chicken chili

For a change of pace, try this distinctive white bean chili. Serve with corn bread or warmed flour tortillas.

ingredients

1 yellow onion, quartered

1 green bell pepper, quartered, seeded

2 tablespoons tomato sauce

3 cloves garlic

¾ lb. boneless, skinless uncooked chicken breast, cut in 2-inch cubes

2 tablespoons olive oil

kosher salt and pepper to taste

1 tablespoon ground cumin

2 teaspoons dried oregano

1 teaspoon ground red chile pepper

3 cans cannellini beans, 2 cans drained

3 cups low-sodium chicken broth

2 (4 ounces) cans diced green chiles

½ cup shredded cheddar cheese, garnish

2 tablespoons fresh chopped cilantro, garnish

directions

1. Place the onion, bell pepper and garlic into the 40-ounce Processor Bowl. PULSE, using short pulses, until finely chopped. Remove and set aside.

2. Add the cubed chicken to the 40-ounce Processor Bowl. PULSE, using long pulses, until finely ground.

3. Heat the oil in a large saucepan over medium heat. Add the chopped onion mixture and saute 5 minutes, until soft.

4. Add the ground chicken along with salt, pepper, cumin, oregano, and chile flakes. Cook 5 minutes, then add the 2 cans of drained beans, green chiles and chicken broth.

5. Place remaining can of beans with the liquid into a clean 40-ounce Processor Bowl. PULSE, using long pulses, until smooth. Add to the chili and simmer 30 to 40 minutes, until slightly thickened.

6. Adjust seasoning and serve, garnished with cheese and cilantro.

PREP TIME: 15 minutes   MAKES: 2 servings   CONTAINER: 40-ounce Processor Bowl

chopped salad with garbanzo beans

Filling & flavorful, this will make frequent appearances in your lunch box.

ingredients

⅓ cup chopped radicchio

½ cup loosely packed parsley

½ cup loosely packed watercress

½ cup bibb lettuce

¼ red pepper, cut in half

¼ cup feta

10 grape tomatoes

¾ cup canned garbanzo beans, drained and blotted dry

Kosher salt and pepper to taste

4 tablespoons favorite salad dressing

directions

1. Place all ingredients into the 40-ounce Processor Bowl in the order listed.

2. PULSE using short pulses, until desired chop. Toss with your favorite salad dressing and enjoy!

PREP TIME: 15 minutes COOK TIME: 20 minutes   MAKES: 4 servings CONTAINER: 40-ounce Processor Bowl

cauliflower cous cous

Cauliflower and other cruciferous vegetables support our bodies' detox system.

ingredients

3 cups cauliflower florets

1 tablespoon chopped rosemary

1 clove garlic, minced

2 teaspoons lemon juice

¼ cup extra-virgin olive oil

½ teaspoon kosher salt

½ teaspoon ground black pepper

½ cup sliced almonds

¼ cup sliced green onion

directions

1. Preheat oven to 400°F. Place the cauliflower into the Processor Bowl. PULSE, using short pulses, until finely chopped.

2. Lay out chopped cauliflower in a single layer on a baking sheet and roast 5 to 10 minutes, until just golden brown.

3. Transfer cauliflower to a mixing bowl and add the rosemary, garlic, lemon juice, olive oil, salt, black pepper, almonds, and green onion. Toss to combine.

NINJA KNOW-HOW PULSE AND GENTLY CHOP WHOLE ALMONDS IN YOUR NINJA® PROCESSOR BOWL IF YOU DON'T HAVE SLICED ALMONDS.

PREP TIME: 30 minutes   MARINADE TIME: 2 hours   COOK TIME: 4 minutes   MAKES: 4 servings   CONTAINER: 40-ounce Processor Bowl

chicken pita sandwich

An easy, high-protein dinner in less than 30 minutes with scrumptious, ethnic flavors.

ingredients

1 lb. uncooked chicken breast, cut in 2-inch cubes

¼ cup Tandoori Marinade (see page 112)

4 (8 inch) whole wheat pita bread rounds

2 vine ripe tomatoes, sliced

8 Boston lettuce leaves

⅓ cup Cucumber Feta Dip (see page 166)

directions

1. Marinate the cubed chicken for 2 hours in the Tandoori Marinade.

2. Place the chicken into the 40-ounce Processor Bowl and PULSE until finely chopped.

3. Lightly coat a nonstick skillet with vegetable cooking cooking spray and place over medium heat. Add the ground chicken and saute for 4 minutes, until cooked through.

4. To assemble sandwich, cut pita bread rounds in half, open the pocket, place the lettuce and tomato in, and evenly divide the cucumber feta dip and cooked ground chicken into the pockets.

chicken enchiladas

A flavorful and healthy dinner idea to create a midweek fiesta for the family!

ingredients

½ medium yellow onion, quartered

2 cloves garlic

1 can (14.5 ounces) diced tomato

1 tablespoon chili powder

1 can (4 ounces) can diced green chilies

1 teaspoon ground cumin

1 tablespoon oregano leaves

1 tablespoon lemon juice

¼ teaspoon kosher salt

½ teaspoon ground black pepper

1 lb. boneless chicken breast, cut in 2-inch cubes

1 tablespoon olive oil

10 (6 inch) corn tortillas

2 cups shredded low-fat cheddar cheese

1 can (15.5 ounces) can black beans, rinsed and drained

Olive oil misto spray

½ cup chopped cilantro

directions

ENCHILADA SAUCE

1. Place the onion, garlic, diced tomato, chili powder, green chilies, cumin, oregano, lemon juice, salt, and black pepper into the 16-ounce Chopper.

2. PULSE until desired consistency, using short pulses. Set aside.

CHICKEN

1. Place the chicken into the 40-ounce Food Processor Bowl.

2. PULSE until desired consistency, using short pulses.

3. Heat the oil in a medium saucepan over medium heat and sauté the ground chicken for 6 to 8 minutes or until cooked.

ASSEMBLY

1. Preheat oven to 350°F. Spray 9x9-inch baking dish with olive oil misto spray.

2. To assemble tortillas, layer 2 tablespoons cooked chicken, 3 tablespoons black beans, and 2 tablespoons shredded cheese, in the center of each tortilla. Roll up each tortilla, and place in 9x9-inch baking dish. Once all tortillas are assembled, pour the enchilada sauce over the tortillas and sprinkle with remaining cheese.

3. Bake at 350°F uncovered, for 25 minutes, or until hot. Remove from oven and garnish with chopped cilantro. Serve immediately.

135

PREP TIME: 15 minutes   COOK TIME: 1 hour   MAKES: 6 servings   CONTAINER: 40-ounce Processor Bowl

chicken pot pie

Sprouts are a great way to get lots of extra micronutrients into your diet.

ingredients

CRUST

Crust (recipe page 194)

FILLING

4 carrots, peeled, cut in thirds

3 celery stalks, cut in thirds

1½ small onions, quartered

1 lb. boneless, skinless, uncooked chicken breast, cut in 2-inch cubes

2 tablespoons olive oil

4 tablespoons butter

4 tablespoons flour

2 cups low sodium chicken broth

1 tablespoon fresh thyme sprigs

Kosher salt and pepper

2 tablespoons milk

directions

1. For Crust: see recipe directions on page 194. Chill dough 1 hour before using.

2. For Filling: Preheat oven to 375°F. Place carrots, celery, and onion into the 40-ounce Processor Bowl and PULSE, using short pulses, until coarsely chopped. Remove chopped vegetables from Processor Bowl and set aside.

3. Place cubed chicken into the 40-ounce Processor Bowl and PULSE, using long pulses, until roughly chopped. Remove and set aside.

4. Heat the oil in a large saucepan over medium heat. Add the chopped vegetables and cook 2 to 3 minutes, until aromatic. Add the chopped chicken and cook, 3 to 4 minutes.

5. Add the butter to the saucepan and melt. Stir in the flour and cook for 3 minutes, until slightly golden brown. Whisk in the chicken broth and bring to a boil, stirring constantly, until mixture starts to thicken. Turn heat to low and simmer for 10 minutes. Add fresh thyme and season with salt and pepper.

6. Pour filling into a 4-quart casserole dish. Remove crust from refrigerator and roll out 2 inches, in diameter, larger than the casserole dish. Place crust on top of filling and crimp as desired. Cut vent holes in crust and brush with milk. Cook for 45 to 50 minutes, until crust is lightly browned.

greek pizza night

Make everything in your Ninja®. Nothing beats homemade pizza from scratch.

ingredients

PIZZA DOUGH

1 packet (¼ ounce) active dry yeast

1 teaspoon sugar

1¼ cups warm water (105–110°F)

4 cups all-purpose flour

1 teaspoon salt

½ cup olive oil

Reserved flour

Reserved water

TOPPINGS

your favorite pizza sauce

1½ cups low-fat mozzarella cheese

1 cup broccoli florets, fresh or frozen

1 cup thinly sliced red pepper

¼ cup sliced black olives

½ cup crumbled feta cheese

directions

1. For dough: Combine the yeast, sugar, and warm water in a small bowl and set aside until foamy, about 5 minutes.

2. Using the single dough blade, place the flour, salt, olive oil, and the yeast mixture into the 40-ounce Food Processor Bowl. PULSE three times, using short pulses, then BLEND for 30 seconds, until dough comes together and forms a ball. Place one ball into a lightly oiled bowl. Cover loosely with plastic wrap and allow to rest and rise for 1 hour, until dough is doubled in size. Wrap the second ball in plastic wrap and freeze for up to 2 months.

3. Preheat oven to 375°F. Lightly spray a cookie sheet with nonstick spray and place the prepared pizza dough. Gently and evenly flatten out the dough all the way to the edges and ½ inch up the edge to form a crust.

4. Spoon your favorite pizza sauce evenly onto the dough, then top with mozzarella cheese, broccoli, red peppers, olives, and feta.

5. Bake for 20 to 25 minutes, checking halfway through, until crust is golden brown.Enjoy with steamed broccoli on the side.

NINJA KNOW-HOW — USE HEALTHY VEGETABLES AND EVEN YOUR FAVORITE FRUIT FOR TOPPINGS TOO.

taco tuesday

A fun and simple family favorite! So simple to make freshly ground meats packed with delicious savory flavors in seconds!

ingredients

1 lb. uncooked, boneless turkey breast, cut in 2-inch cubes

½ medium yellow onion, quartered

1 tablespoon canola oil

1-ounce package low sodium taco seasoning mix

8 hard taco shells

1 cup shredded lettuce

½ cup shredded low-fat cheddar cheese

¼ cup sliced jalapeños

⅓ cup chopped cilantro

Best Blender Salsa, page 164

directions

1. Place the cubed turkey and onion into the 40-ounce Food Processor Bowl.

2. PULSE until finely ground, using short pulses.

3. Heat the oil in a medium skillet over medium heat. Add the ground turkey mixture and cook, stirring occasionally, 6 to 8 minutes, until cooked through. Add the taco seasoning and stir to combine.

4. Assemble each taco with the cooked turkey, lettuce, cheese, jalapeños, cilantro and Best Blender Salsa page 164.

NINJA KNOW-HOW

CHANGE IT UP BY USING BONELESS CHICKEN BREAST, SALMON, OR SHRIMP!

EASY MEAL MAKING

EASY MEAL MAKING

weeknight burger bar

Make delicious fresh burgers in seconds!

ingredients

1 lb. uncooked lean strip steak beef, cut in 2-inch cubes

Salt and pepper to taste

1 tablespoon canola oil

4 whole wheat hamburger buns

4 leaves leaf lettuce

4 slices tomato

4 slices low-fat cheddar cheese

directions

1. Place the cubed beef into the 40-ounce Food Processor Bowl.

2. PULSE, using short pulses, until finely ground.

3. Form into four burgers. Season with salt and ground black pepper.

4. Heat the oil in a medium saucepan over medium-high heat. Cook the burgers to desired internal temperature, 4 minutes per side for medium or 3 minutes per side for medium rare. .

5. Serve on a whole wheat bun with lettuce, tomato and sliced cheese or on a bed of your favorite greens with our ketchup relish page 110.

NINJA KNOW-HOW FOR A DIFFERENT FLAVOR, ADD 2 TABLESPOONS WORCESTERSHIRE, ¼ MEDIUM YELLOW ONION OR 1 TABLESPOON OF STEAK SEASONING WHILE PULSING THE BEEF.

teriyaki tofu stir-fry

Sprouts are a great way to get lots of extra micronutrients into your diet.

ingredients

MARINADE

1 cup fresh pineapple chunks

2 cloves garlic

½-inch piece fresh ginger, peeled

⅓ cup water

¼ cup reduced sodium soy sauce

¼ cup light brown sugar

STIR-FRY

14 ounces extra firm tofu, cut in
2-inch chunks

½ cup sliced button mushrooms

1 cup broccoli florets

½ red bell pepper, thinly sliced

⅛ medium yellow onion, thinly
sliced

1 tablespoon canola oil

2 green onions, thinly sliced

directions

MARINADE

1. Place the pineapple, garlic, ginger, water, soy sauce, and brown sugar into the 16-ounce Chopper in the order listed.

2. PULSE until desired consistency, using short pulses.

STIR FRY

1. Place the tofu in a storage container and pour over marinade. Stir to coat. Place in the refrigerator and marinate for 4 hours.

2. Remove the tofu from marinade, place in bowl, then discard the marinade.

3. Heat the oil in a medium saucepan over medium-high heat and sauté the tofu for 6 to 8 minutes. Add the chopped vegetables and continue to cook for 5 to 7 minutes or until tender. Garnish with chopped scallions. Serve immediately.

PREP TIME: 15 minutes   COOK TIME: 20–25 minutes   MAKES: 16 mini meatballs   CONTAINER: 40-ounce Processor Bowl

turkey meatballs

Serve these small bites to your friends as an appetizer or to your family as a quick and delicious meal.

ingredients

½ lb. uncooked turkey breast, cut into 2-inch cubes

¼ onion

2 cloves garlic, minced

2 tablespoons chopped fresh parsley

¼ cup grated parmesan cheese

2 tablespoons bread crumbs

1 tablespoon tomato paste

1 egg, beaten

Salt and pepper to taste

Cooking spray

2 cups Sundried Tomato Sauce, page 111

vegetable cooking spray

directions

1. Place the cubed turkey and the onion into the 40-ounce Processor Bowl. PULSE, using long pulses, until finely ground.

2. Transfer the ground turkey to a bowl and add garlic, parsley, cheese, bread crumbs, tomato paste, egg, salt, and pepper. Mix to combine then form into 16 small meatballs.

3. Heat a large skillet over medium-high and lightly spray with vegetable cooking spray. Add the meatballs and brown on all sides, about 5 minutes. Add marinara sauce and simmer 20 to 25 minutes until meatballs are cooked through completely. Serve atop your favorite pasta.

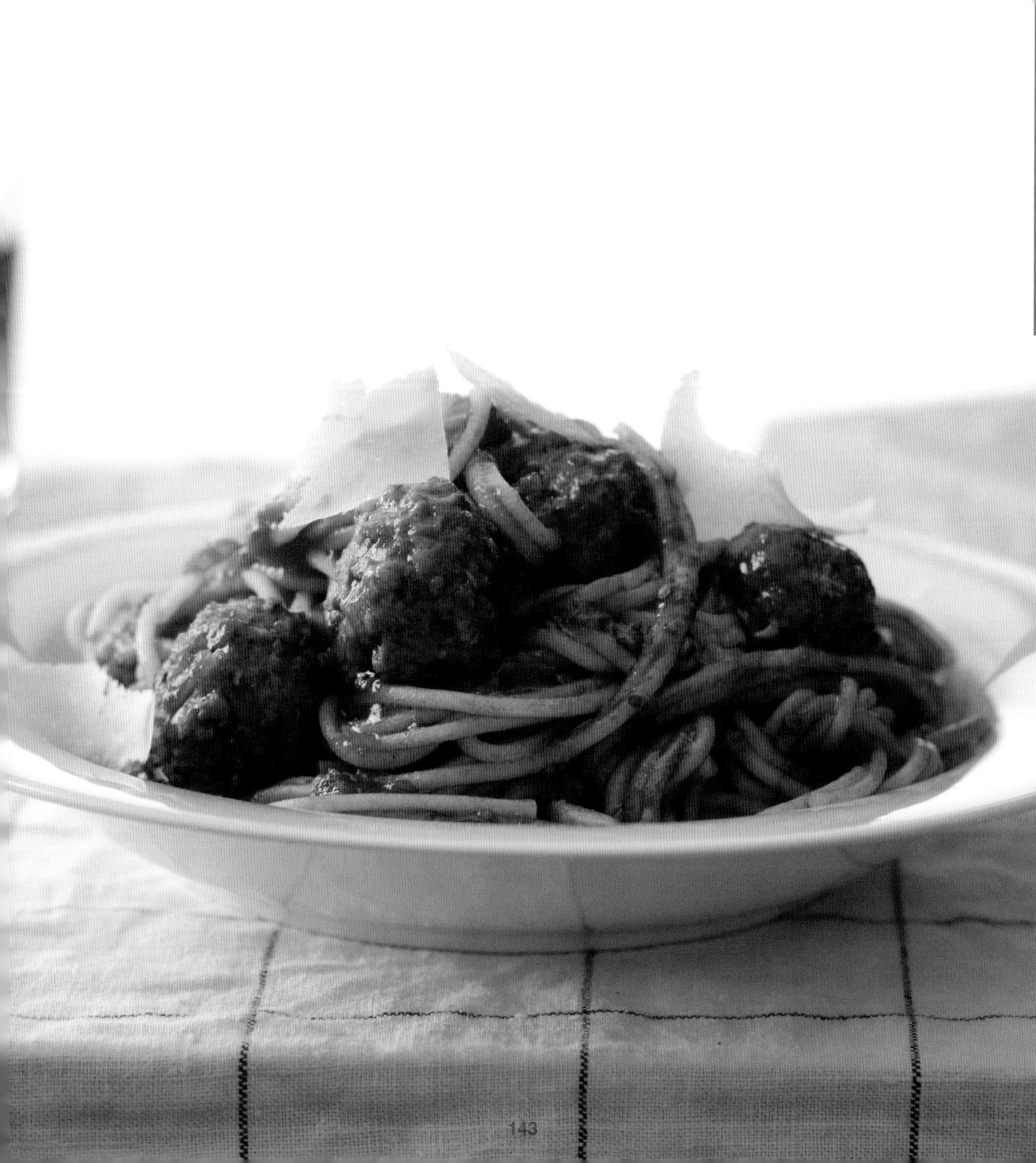

PREP TIME: 20 minutes   COOK TIME: 30 minutes   MAKES: 10 servings   CONTAINER: 40-ounce Processor Bowl

vegetable chili casserole

The kidney beans in this chili are a great source of fiber and protein!

ingredients

1 medium zucchini, quartered

1 small carrot, peeled, quartered

½ medium yellow onion, halved

½ medium green pepper, halved

2 cloves garlic

¼ teaspoon crushed red pepper

1 teaspoon chipotle in adobo sauce

1 tablespoon vegetable oil

1 tablespoon ground cumin

1 tablespoon ground coriander

2 tablespoons chili powder

1 teaspoon dried oregano

1 can (15.5 oz) red kidney beans, drained

1 can (28 oz) crushed tomatoes

½ teaspoon kosher salt

½ teaspoon ground black pepper

½ lb. cooked macaroni

1½ cups shredded cheddar cheese

½ cup sour cream, optional

vegetable cooking spray

directions

1. Preheat oven to 350°F. Lightly spray a 9x13-inch baking dish with vegetable cooking spray; set aside.

2. Place the zucchini, carrot, onion, bell pepper, garlic, pepper flakes, and chipotle into the 40-ounce Processor Bowl in the order listed. PULSE until finely chopped, using long pulses.

3. Heat oil in a medium saucepan over medium-high heat. Add the vegetable mixture and cook until lightly browned.

4. Add the cumin, coriander, chili powder, oregano, beans, tomatoes, pasta, salt, and pepper and bring to a boil. Pour the chili into the prepared baking dish and bake for 30 minutes. Remove from oven, top with shredded cheese, then return to oven for 5 additional minutes.

5. Serve with a side of sour cream, if desired.

coconut macadamia crusted shrimp

This delicious homemade crust also tastes great with Halibut and Mahi Mahi.

ingredients

½ cup of unsweetened coconut flakes

½ cup macadamia nuts

4 slices of dry stale or lightly toasted bread

¼ teaspoon salt

1 egg

¾ cup coconut milk

2 cups flour

1 lb. uncooked, peeled, deveined shrimp (16/20 ct.)

4 tablespoons honey

1 tablespoon Dijon mustard

vegetable cooking spray

directions

1. Preheat oven to 425°F. Place a roasting rack on a sheet tray and set aside.

2. Place coconut flakes, macadamia nuts, bread and salt into the 16-ounce Chopper in the order listed.

3. PULSE 5 to 7 times, using long pulses, until mixture is coarsely ground; pour into a medium dish. Set aside.

4. In medium mixing bowl beat egg and milk together. Set aside.

5. Lightly dust shrimp with the flour, then immerse into the egg/milk mixture, and then roll in the macadamia coating.

6. Place the coated shrimp on the roasting rack. Lightly spray the shrimp with olive oil.

7. Bake for 10 to 15 minutes or until golden brown. While baking, combine the honey and Dijon mustard in a small bowl. Serve immediately. Serve sauce with shrimp.

EASY MEAL MAKING

coconut chicken with orange sauce

Light coconut milk is lower in calories and gives a rich texture and nutty sweetness.

ingredients

1 can (14 ounces) light coconut milk

2 cloves garlic

½ teaspoon kosher salt

2 tablespoons green curry paste

4 6-ounce uncooked, boneless, skinless chicken breasts

½ cup orange marmalade

2 tablespoons prepared horseradish

Cornstarch, to coat

¼ cup vegetable oil

4 cups steamed broccoli

directions

1. Place the coconut milk, garlic, salt, and curry paste into the 16-ounce Chopper and BLEND until smooth.

2. In an airtight container, place the chicken and coconut mixture and marinate for 12 hours.

3. Preheat oven to 375°F. Lightly spray a baking sheet with vegetable cooking spray; set aside.

4. In a mixing bowl, combine the marmalade and horseradish.

5. Remove chicken and drain excess marinade. Coat chicken in cornstarch.

6. Heat the oil in a medium skillet over medium-high heat. Add the chicken and cook 2 minutes per side, until golden brown. Remove chicken and place on prepared baking sheet.

7. Bake for 10 minutes or until thoroughly cooked through. To serve, place one chicken breast on a plate and drizzle with orange sauce. Enjoy with steamed broccoli on the side.

EASY MEAL MAKING

almond crusted chicken

. . . .

Almonds add texture and a lot of flavor to traditional bread crumbs. Try using only almond meal for a completely gluten-free option.

ingredients

¾ cup raw almonds

¼ cup breadcrumbs

2 cloves garlic

½ teaspoon paprika

¼ teaspoon onion powder

½ teaspoon kosher salt

¼ teaspoon ground black pepper

4 uncooked, boneless, skinless chicken breasts

1 egg white, beaten

directions

1. Preheat oven to 400°F. Lightly spray a baking sheet with vegetable cooking spray; set aside.

2. Place the almonds, breadcrumbs, garlic, paprika, onion powder, salt, and pepper into the 16-ounce Chopper in the order listed.

3. PULSE 7 to 10 times, using long pulses, until finely ground. Transfer almond breading to a shallow dish.

4. Dip the chicken breasts in the egg white then coat in the almond breading. Place onto the prepared baking sheet and bake 20 to 25 minutes, until no longer pink in the center.

NINJA KNOW-HOW : SERVE ATOP A BED OF MIXED GREENS WITH THE PASSION FRUIT VINAIGRETTE (PAGE 115)

PREP TIME: 15 minutes   COOK TIME: 30 minutes   MAKES: 4 servings   CONTAINER: 40-ounce Processor Bowl

gluten-free spanish veggie burgers

The quinoa with the cilantro and cumin makes for a yummy vegetable burger.

ingredients

1 can (15½ ounces) black beans, drained

¼ medium onion

2 cloves garlic

1 large egg, beaten

1 cup cooked quinoa

1 lime, juiced

1 tablespoon ground cumin

½ cup cilantro leaves, chopped

⅔ cup textured vegetable protein, rehydrated

½ cup gluten-free bread crumbs

½ teaspoon kosher salt

½ teaspoon ground black pepper

directions

1. Place the black beans, onion, garlic, and egg into the 40-ounce Processor Bowl and PULSE to finely chop.

2. Transfer chopped ingredients to a mixing bowl, then add the quinoa, lime juice, cumin, cilantro, vegetable protein, bread crumbs, salt, and black pepper, mixing to combine. Form mixture into 6 burgers.

3. Lightly coat a large skillet with cooking spray. Over medium-high heat, sauté burgers until browned on both sides and heated through, about 12 minutes.

NINJA KNOW-HOW MAKE BURGERS AHEAD OF TIME. SIMPLY WRAP THEM IN PLASTIC WRAP AND FREEZE FOR FUTURE USE.

PREP TIME: 15 minutes   COOK TIME: 25 minutes   MAKES: 4 servings   CONTAINER: 40-ounce Processor Bowl

pork chops with peach chutney

Peaches are an often-overlooked tasty combination with pork.

ingredients

½ medium onion

1 tablespoon ginger, peeled

½ jalapeño, seeded

1½ cups sliced, ripe peaches

2 tablespoons lime juice

1 tablespoon agave nectar

2 teaspoons red wine vinegar

¼ teaspoon kosher salt

¼ teaspoon ground black pepper

⅛ teaspoon nutmeg

½ cup golden raisins

½ cup fresh parsley leaves

4 bone-in pork chops, cooked

directions

1. Place the onion, ginger, jalapeño, peaches, lime juice, agave nectar, vinegar, salt, black pepper, nutmeg, raisins, and parsley into the 40-ounce Processor Bowl and BLEND to finely chop, scraping sides as needed.

2. Place mixture into a saucepot and simmer for 20 minutes, stirring occasionally.

3. To serve, place one cooked pork chop on a plate with the chutney.

NINJA KNOW-HOW : THIS CHUTNEY IS EQUALLY DELICIOUS SERVED WITH CHICKEN OR TURKEY.

PREP TIME: 15 minutes   COOK TIME: 25 minutes   MAKES: 4 servings   CONTAINER: 40-ounce Processor Bowl

asian pork meatballs

Recent studies suggest that the fermentation process used to make soy sauce creates unique carbohydrates called oligosaccharides that help in the digestion of the food it seasons.

ingredients

1 lb. uncooked pork tenderloin, cut in 2-inch cubes

2 cloves garlic

½-inch piece fresh ginger, peeled

4 green onions, sliced, divided

2 tablespoons low-sodium soy sauce

1 teaspoon ground coriander

1 large egg

Juice of 1 lime

½ cup fresh pineapple chunks

1 tablespoon whole-grain mustard

½ cup unseasoned bread crumbs

2 cups sweet-and sour-sauce, store-bought, warmed

directions

1. Preheat oven to 350°F.

2. Place the pork, garlic, ginger, scallion, soy sauce, coriander, egg, lime juice, pineapple, mustard, and bread crumbs into the 40-ounce Processor Bowl and PULSE to finely chop.

3. Form into small meatballs. Bake on a sheet pan for 15 minutes or until cooked.

4. Pour warm sweet and sour sauce over meatballs in a serving bowl. Garnish with scallions.

stuffed peppers with beef & quinoa

This is a simple, complete meal that will become a go-to favorite.

ingredients

½ medium onion

2 stalks celery, cut in thirds

2 cloves garlic

1½ lbs. uncooked lean beef, cut in 2-inch cubes

1 tablespoon vegetable oil

1 large egg

½ teaspoon kosher salt

½ teaspoon ground black pepper

¾ cup cooked quinoa

1¼ cups tomato sauce

2 large green peppers, cut in half, seeded

1½ cups shredded mozzarella cheese

directions

1. Preheat oven to 350°F. Place the onion, celery, and garlic into the 40-ounce Processor Bowl and PULSE to finely chop, scraping sides as needed. Remove vegetables and set aside.

2. In the same Processor Bowl, place the beef and PULSE to finely chop.

3. In a nonstick sauté pan, heat the oil over medium-high heat. Add the beef and cook until evenly browned, stirring occasionally. Discard fat.

4. Transfer chopped vegetables and cooked beef to a mixing bowl, then add the egg, salt, black pepper, cooked quinoa, and tomato sauce. Mix to combine. Fill each of the pepper halves with the beef mixture.

5. Lightly coat a baking dish with cooking spray and place the stuffed peppers in. Cover with tin foil and bake for 1 hour. Top with cheese and continue to cook for 5 minutes or until cheese is melted.

PREP TIME: 15 minutes   COOK TIME: 25 minutes   MAKES: 4 servings   CONTAINER: 40-ounce Processor Bowl

stuffed flounder creole

This recipe will be a big hit with your family, well worth the bit of extra work.

ingredients

½ medium onion

1 celery stalk, cut in thirds

½ medium green bell pepper, chopped

1 clove garlic

1 lb. uncooked, peeled, deveined shrimp

¾ cup buttery crackers

1 tablespoon vegetable oil

1 tablespoon Dijon mustard

3 dashes hot sauce

2 teaspoons lemon juice

2 teaspoons Creole seasoning

1 tablespoon tomato paste

4 (6 ounce) flounder fillets

directions

1. Preheat oven to 350°F. Lightly coat a baking sheet with cooking spray; set aside.

2. Place the onion, celery, green pepper, and garlic into the 40-ounce Processor Bowl and PULSE, using short pulses, until finely chopped. Remove mixture and set aside.

3. In the same 40-ounce Processor Bowl, place the shrimp and crackers and PULSE, using short pulses, until finely chopped.

4. Heat oil in a medium skillet over medium heat. Add the vegetable mix and saute 5 minutes, until translucent.

5. Place cooked vegetable mixture and raw shrimp mixture in a mixing bowl, then add the mustard, hot sauce, lemon juice, Creole seasoning, and tomato paste.

6. Lay flounder flat on prep area and add equally divide the stuffing. Roll flounder to cover then lay on the prepared baking sheet. Bake for 20 minutes or until flounder and stuffing is cooked through.

gnocchi with mediterranean pesto

Pine nuts contain pinoleic acid, which makes you feel fuller faster. They are also rich in vitamin A and lutein, both of which are known to support sharper vision.

ingredients

2 cloves garlic

2 cups fresh basil leaves

½ cup toasted pine nuts

¼ cup cubed parmesan cheese

1 cup extra-virgin olive oil

¼ cup pitted green olives

¼ teaspoon ground black pepper

2 lbs. gnocchi, cooked,
kept warm

¾ cup sun-dried tomatoes, sliced

½ cup crumbled feta cheese

directions

1. Place the garlic, basil, pine nuts, parmesan cheese, olive oil, olives, and black pepper into the 40-ounce Processor Bowl and PULSE using short pulses, to finely chop, scraping sides as needed.

2. Pour sauce into saucepan, add the warm gnocchi and sun-dried tomatoes, and simmer until heated through.

3. To serve, ladle gnocchi into a bowl and top with feta cheese.

EASY MEAL MAKING

PREP TIME: 10 minutes   COOK TIME: 40 minutes   MAKES: 6 servings   CONTAINER: 40-ounce Processor Bowl

barbecue turkey shepherd's pie

Turkey is among a group of high-protein foods that can help keep post-meal insulin levels within a desirable range. This tasty dish is well balanced with only 320 calories.

ingredients

2 cloves garlic

1 celery stalk, cut in thirds

1 medium carrot, peeled, cut in thirds

½ medium onion, quartered

2 tablespoons vegetable oil

2 tablespoons flour

1 cup low-sodium turkey broth, heated

1 cup barbecue sauce

¼ teaspoon kosher salt

¾ teaspoon ground black pepper

1½ lbs. cooked turkey breast, cut in 2-inch cubes

1¼ cups thawed frozen peas

3 cups mashed potatoes, heated

directions

1. Preheat oven to 375°F.

2. Place the garlic, celery, carrot, and onion into the 40-ounce Processor Bowl and PULSE using short pulses, to finely chop.

3. Heat oil in a medium saucepan over medium heat. Add the chopped vegetable mixture and saute until softened, 5 to 7 minutes.

4. Add the flour, stirring to coat the vegetables.

5. Slowly whisk in the broth, then add the barbecue sauce, salt, black pepper, and turkey. Cook for 10 minutes until sauce thickens. Stir in peas.

6. Pour mixture into a 9x9-inch baking dish and spread the mashed potatoes on top to cover turkey mixture. Bake for 30 minutes or until heated through.

EASY MEAL MAKING

salmon burgers

This burger is a new creative spin to get an additional serving of fish into your diet during the week....and it's so easy too!

ingredients

2 green onions, cut in thirds

1¼ lbs. uncooked, boneless, skinless salmon, cut in 2-inch chunks

2 teaspoons Dijon mustard

1 tablespoon lemon juice

1 large egg

¾ teaspoon Old Bay® seasoning

½ teaspoon ground black pepper

¼ cup panko bread crumbs

directions

1. Place all ingredients into the 40-ounce Processor Bowl in the order listed then PULSE using short pulses, until finely ground. Form into four equal burgers.

2. Spray a nonstick skillet or grill pan with vegetable cooking spray and place over medium-high heat. Add burgers and cook until golden brown on outside and cooked through, about 3 minutes per side.

3. Serve on a whole wheat bun with lettuce and tomato, or on a bed of your favorite greens.

entertaining

hummus

. . . .

Adding roasted red peppers, olives, or roasted garlic will give this recipe your own personal twist. Enjoy with homemade pita chips or fresh vegetable crudites!

ingredients

2 cups cooked, drained garbanzo
beans (liquid reserved)

¼ cup + 2 tablespoons garbanzo
bean liquid

¼ cup lemon juice

¼ cup tablespoon olive oil

1 clove garlic

⅛ cup tahini

1 teaspoon ground cumin

½ teaspoon kosher salt

directions

1. Place all ingredients into the 40-ounce Processor Bowl, in the order listed above, starting with the garbanzo beans.

2. BLEND until smooth.

PREP TIME: 20 minutes   COOK TIME: 35 minutes   MAKES: 10–12 servings   CONTAINER: 40-ounce Processor Bowl

chorizo taco dip

Extremely rich and delicious, even using the low-fat cream cheese.

ingredients

1 lb. chorizo, chopped

½ medium onion

1 green bell pepper, quartered, seeded

1 tablespoon vegetable oil

1 package (8 ounces) low-fat cream cheese

½ cup low-fat ranch dressing

1 cup salsa

1 cup shredded Colby Jack cheese

1 package (1 ounce) low sodium taco seasoning

1 cup sliced black olives

directions

1. Preheat oven to 350°F.

2. Place the chorizo, onion, and green pepper into the 40-ounce Processor Bowl. PULSE until desired chop.

3. Heat oil in a medium skillet over medium-high heat. Add the chorizo mix and saute until vegetables are tender, about 5 minutes. Place mixture into a mixing bowl.

4. Place the cream cheese, ranch dressing, salsa, cheese, and taco seasoning into the the 40-ounce Processor Bowl and BLEND until smooth.

5. Add the cream cheese mixture and black olives to the chorizo mixture, stirring to combine.

6. Place mixture into a 9x9-inch baking dish. Bake for 25 minutes or until bubbly hot.

NINJA KNOW-HOW — SUBSTITUTE CHICKEN SAUSAGE FOR LOWER FAT AND CALORIES.

161

tabbouleh

This dip contains parsley, a herb with the same amount of vitamin C as an orange.
Plus, it's gluten-free!

ingredients

¼ English cucumber, quartered

¼ small yellow onion, peeled,
halved

2 tablespoons fresh mint leaves

½ cup loosely packed flat leaf
parsley leaves

1½ vine-ripe tomatoes, quartered

¼ teaspoon ground black pepper

¼ teaspoon kosher salt

1 tablespoon extra-virgin olive oil

1 tablespoon freshly
squeezed lemon juice

directions

1. Place all ingredients into the 16-ounce Chopper in the order listed.

2. PULSE until desired consistency is reached.

NINJA KNOW-HOW | SERVE THIS AS AN ACCOMPANIMENT TO GRILLED FISH, BEEF, OR LAMB.

ENTERTAINING

best blender salsa

. . . .

You can depend on the flavor of this salsa every time! Canned tomatoes create consistency and rich flavor.

ingredients

1 can (14 ounces) whole peeled
tomatoes

¼ cup fresh cilantro leaves

½ white onion, quartered

½ jalapeño, seeded

½ chipotle chile

1 tablespoon adobo sauce

½ lime, peeled, quartered

Kosher salt and pepper, to taste

directions

1. Place all ingredients into the 40-ounce Processor Bowl in the
order listed.

2. PULSE to desired consistency.

 NINJA KNOW-HOW | FOR A TROPICAL VARIATION, ADD ½ CUP FRESH MANGO TO THE PROCESSOR BOWL.

PREP TIME: 30 minutes MAKES: 4–6 servings CONTAINER: 16-ounce Chopper

cucumber feta dip

A delicious and light dip perfect with fresh carrots, peppers, and celery sticks!

ingredients

¼ small red onion, halved

½ cup English cucumber, peeled, cut in quarters

¼ cup loosely packed fresh dill

½ cup crumbled feta cheese

1 tablespoon freshly squeezed lemon juice

¼ teaspoon ground black pepper

directions

1. Place all ingredients into the 16-ounce Chopper in the order listed.

2. PULSE 8 to 10 times, using short pulses.

NINJA KNOW-HOW — ADD ¼ CUP CELERY TOPS AND LEAVES FOR EXTRA CRUNCH AND NUTRIENTS.

PREP TIME: 10 minutes   MAKES: 4 servings   CONTAINER: 16-ounce Chopper

pimento cheese dip

A perfect healthier dip to be served with your favorite fresh vegetables—carrots, celery, and broccoli florets!

ingredients

4 ounces 1/3 less fat cream cheese

1/2 cup shredded low-fat cheddar cheese

2 tablespoons nonfat plain Greek yogurt

1/4 teaspoon kosher salt

1/4 teaspoon onion powder

2 ounces drained pimiento

directions

1. Place the cream cheese, cheddar cheese, yogurt, and onion powder into the 16-ounce Chopper in the order listed.

2. PULSE until desired consistency, using short pulses.

3. Scrape down the sides of the Processor Bowl then add the pimentos. PULSE 8 to 10 times, using short pulses, until pimientos are chopped and combined.

ENTERTAINING

spinach & artichoke dip

Simply delicious served with pita or whole-grain chips.

ingredients

¼ cup mayonnaise

¼ cup sour cream

8 ounces cream cheese

2 tablespoons lemon juice

½ cup shredded low-fat mozzarella cheese

¼ cup grated parmesan

2 cloves garlic

Kosher salt and pepper, to taste

1 can (14 ounces) artichoke hearts, drained

1 cup frozen spinach, thawed, excess liquid removed

directions

1. Preheat oven to 350°F. Place all ingredients, except for the artichokes and spinach, into the 40-ounce Processor Bowl in the order listed. BLEND for 30 seconds, until combined.

2. Add the artichokes and spinach to the creamed mixture and PULSE, using short pulses, 5 to 7 times, until incorporated. Spoon the dip into a heat-resistant serving dish and bake for 20 minutes. Serve with sliced french bread.

PREP TIME: 10 minutes   COOK TIME: 10 minutes   MAKES: 6–8 servings   CONTAINER: 16-ounce Nutri Ninja® Cup

smoked salmon blinis

Capers add bold and vibrant flavor to your meals—the small, pickled flower buds contain mustard oil, so even a few capers impart big taste.

ingredients

¾ cup low-fat milk

1 large egg

1 tablespoon vegetable oil

⅓ cup buckwheat flour

⅔ cup pancake mix, store-bought

½ lb. smoked salmon

2 tablespoons capers

2 tablespoons fresh dill

¼ cup sour cream

directions

1. Place the milk, egg, oil, flour, and pancake mix into the 16-ounce Nutri Ninja® Cup and BLEND until smooth.

2. On a lightly oiled griddle over medium heat, cook batter in desired-size pancakes until small bubbles form and edges dry. Flip and cook until pancake center is puffed and springs back when gently pressed. Top each pancake with smoked salmon, capers, dill, and a dollop of sour cream.

NINJA KNOW-HOW — AN ALTERNATIVE TO SMOKED SALMON COULD BE LOX, BELLY LOX, OR PASTRAMI CURED SALMON.

ENTERTAINING

crab cake sliders

When a quick snack is needed for entertaining, why not make delicious crab cakes that are healthier and not deep fried!

ingredients

3 tablespoons light mayonnaise

1 teaspoon Dijon mustard

1 tablespoon lemon juice

1 large egg

2 teaspoons Old Bay® seasoning

¼ cup chopped roasted red pepper

¼ cup chopped scallion

½ cup unseasoned bread crumbs

1 lb. jumbo lump crabmeat

1 tablespoon olive oil

directions

1. Place the mayonnaise, mustard, lemon juice, egg, Old Bay®. seasoning, red pepper, and scallion into the 16-ounce Chopper and BLEND until smooth.

2. Place the mixture into a mixing bowl and add the bread crumbs and crabmeat, folding mixture gently as to not break up the lumps. Form mixture into six patties.

3. In a nonstick sauté pan, heat the oil over medium-high heat and sauté crab cakes until browned on both sides and heated through, about 10 minutes.

smoky deviled eggs

An entertaining staple with a touch of smoked paprika.

ingredients

12 hard-boiled eggs, peeled

½ cup mayonnaise

¼ teaspoon smoked paprika, plus more for garnish

⅛ teaspoon onion powder

½ teaspoon ground mustard

¼ teaspoon kosher salt

¼ teaspoon ground black pepper

directions

1. Cut eggs in half and remove yolks. Place the yolks into the 16-ounce Chopper.

1. Add remaining ingredients to the 16-ounce Chopper and PULSE 5 to 7 times, using long pulses, until yolk filling is smooth and fluffy.

1. Use a spoon or a pastry bag to stuff the yolk filling into each hard-boiled egg white half.

2. Sprinkle additional smoked paprika over the eggs and serve.

PREP TIME: 5 minutes   MAKES: 3 servings   CONTAINER: 40-ounce Processor Bowl

walk on the beach

. . . .

The fresh grapefruit and lime is much healthier than the pre-mixes filled with corn syrup.

ingredients

½ cup vodka

¼ cup peach schnapps

½ grapefruit, peeled, quartered, seeded

½ lime, peeled

2 tablespoons grenadine

2 cups ice

directions

1. Place all ingredients into the 40-ounce Processor Bowl in the order listed.

2. BLEND until smooth.

NINJA **KNOW-HOW** | YOU CAN SUBSTITUTE 4 OUNCES FRESH OR FROZEN PEACHES FOR THE PEACH SCHNAPPS.

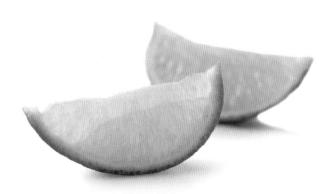

ENTERTAINING

frozen margarita

This summertime party favorite is foolproof!

ingredients

¾ cup tequila

¼ cup triple sec

1/3 cup fresh lime juice

1/3 cup water

¾ cup frozen limeade

2 cups ice

directions

1. Place all ingredients into the 40-ounce Processor Bowl in the order listed.

2. BLEND until smooth.

 NINJA
KNOW-HOW

SUBSTITUTE FROZEN STRAWBERRIES FOR THE ICE IN THIS RECIPE AND MAKE A DELICIOUS STRAWBERRY MARGARITA.

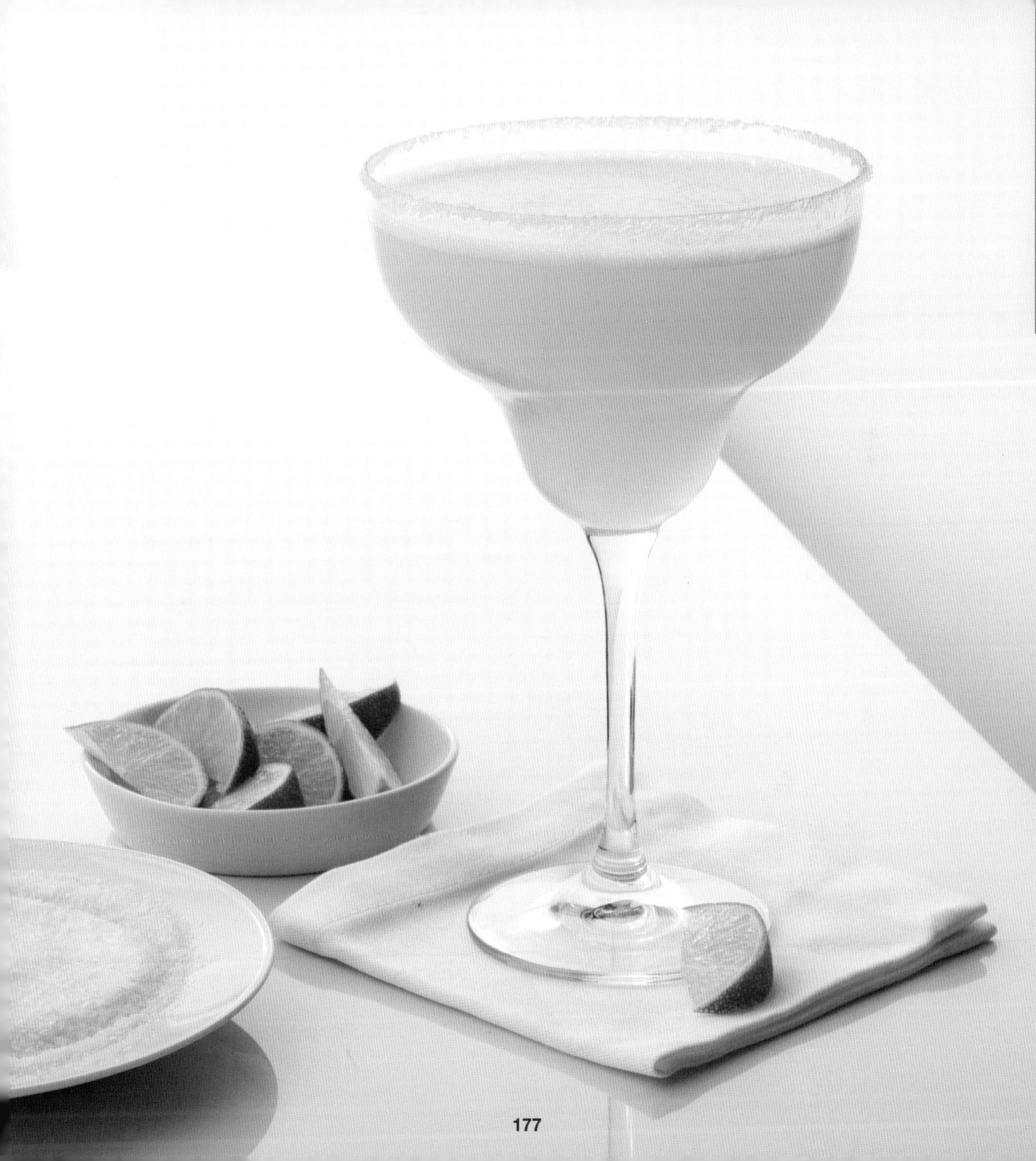

frozen sangria

Try different combinations of your favorite frozen fruits, perfect for entertaining.

ingredients

1¼ cups frozen strawberries

1¼ cups frozen pineapple chunks

1¼ cups frozen peach slices

1 lime, peeled, halved

1 seedless orange, peeled, halved

1¼ cups red wine

¼ cup brandy

directions

1. Place all ingredients into the 40-ounce Processor Bowl in the order listed.

2. PULSE until smooth, using long pulses.

PREP TIME: 5 minutes   MAKES: 4 servings   CONTAINER: 40-ounce Processor Bowl

cool watermelon martini

A fun and refreshing way to enjoy those hot summer nights!

ingredients

2 cups watermelon chunks

3 ounces vodka

2 ounces triple sec

2 tablespoons agave

1½ cups ice

directions

1. Place all ingredients into the 40-ounce Processor Bowl in the order listed above.

2. BLEND until smooth.

3. Serve in chilled martini glasses.

peach bellini

Spoil your guests with this fabulous cocktail when summer fruit is ripe and sweet.

ingredients

2 large ripe peaches, peeled, pitted

3 ounces peach schnapps

10 ounces well-chilled Prosecco

2 cups ice

directions

1. Place all ingredients into the 40-ounce Processor Bowl in the order listed.

2. BLEND until smooth.

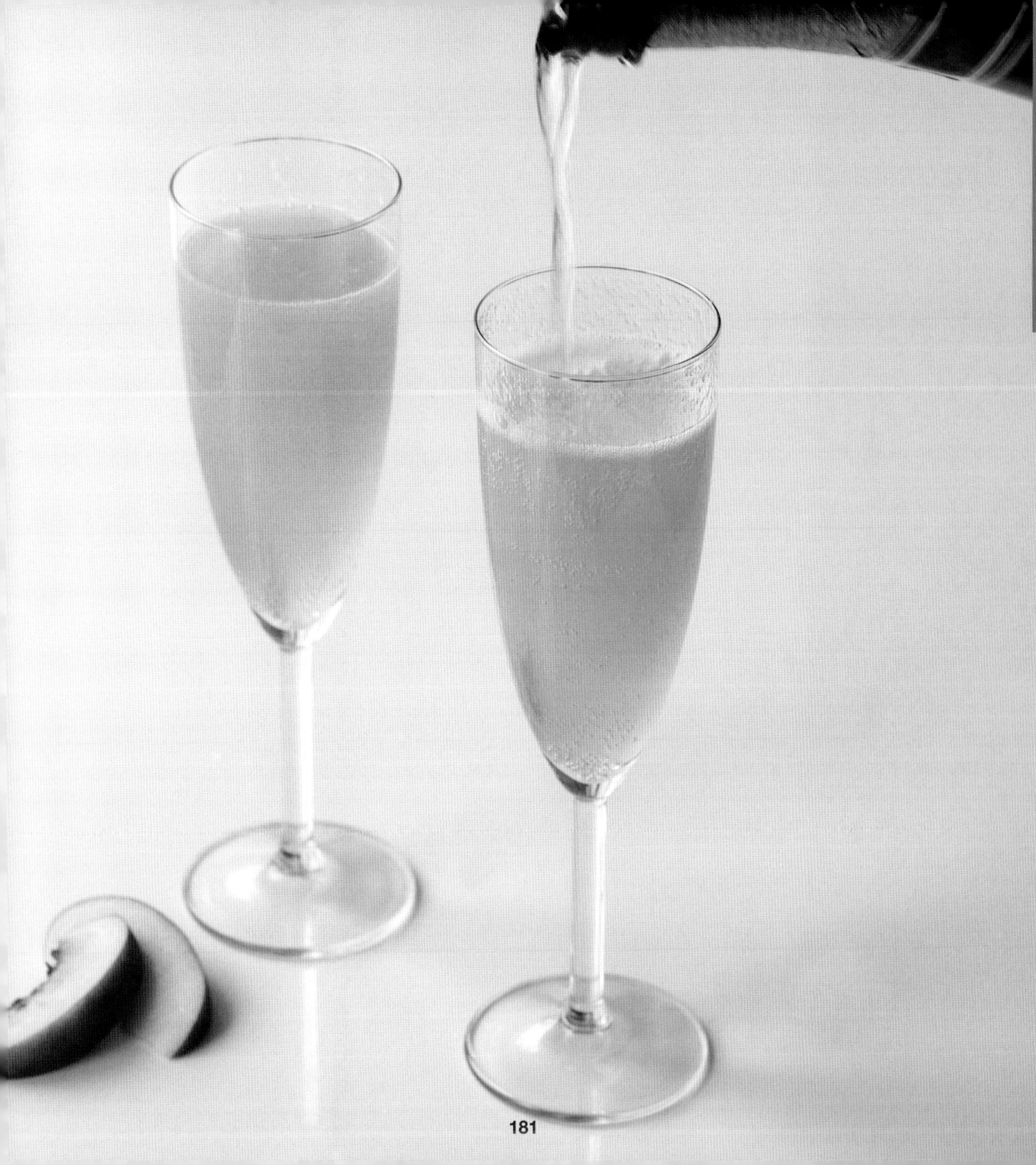

PREP TIME: 5 minutes   MAKES: 2 servings   CONTAINER: 40-ounce Processor Bowl

mudslide

A fun dessert resort-style cocktail perfect for entertaining; your guests will be impressed!

ingredients

2½ cups ice

1¼ ounces vodka

1¾ ounces coffee liqueur

1¾ ounces Irish cream liqueur

1 tablespoon chocolate syrup, plus more for garnish

Whipped cream

directions

1. Place all the ingredients, except the whipped cream, into the 40-ounce Processor Bowl in the order listed.

2. BLEND until smooth.

3. Serve topped with whipped cream and a drizzle of chocolate syrup.

NINJA KNOW-HOW — A DOUBLE SHOT OF CHILLED ESPRESSO MAY BE SUBSTITUTED FOR THE COFFEE LIQUEUR---JUST DOUBLE THE AMOUNT OF IRISH CREAM LIQUEUR.

banana colada

Frozen pineapple, bananas and coconut milk make this indulgent cocktail fresh and delicious.

ingredients

1½ cups frozen pineapple chunks

1½ frozen small bananas

6 ounces light rum

1½ cups pineapple juice

¾ cup light coconut milk

¾ cup ice

directions

1. Place all ingredients into the 40-ounce Processor Bowl in the order listed.

2. BLEND until smooth.

PREP TIME: 5 minutes   MAKES: 2 servings   CONTAINER: 40-ounce Processor Bowl

lem-mosa

. . . .

A fresh, delicious citrus cooler perfect as a palate cleanser.

ingredients

2 lemons, peeled, halved, seeded

3-4 fresh mint leaves

1 tablespoon agave nectar

1 cup sparkling wine

2 cups ice

directions

1. Place all ingredients into the 40-ounce Processor Bowl in the order listed.

2. BLEND until smooth.

 NINJA KNOW-HOW — ADD FRESH RASPBERRIES AS A GARNISH OR BLEND FOR A NEW TWIST.

PREP TIME: 10 minutes MAKES: 2 servings CONTAINER: 40-ounce Processor Bowl

strawberry daiquiri

Fresh strawberries provide the natural sweetness to this cocktail.

ingredients

2 cups ice

1½ cups hulled strawberries

4 ounces light rum

2 tablespoons lime juice

¼ cup sugar

directions

1. Place all ingredients in the 40-ounce Processor Bowl in the order listed.
2. BLEND until smooth.

PREP TIME: 8 minutes   MAKES: 6 servings   CONTAINER: 40-ounce Processor Bowl

classic bloody mary

A simple and spicy brunch cocktail filled with great flavors—serve with a fresh celery stalk, lemon quarter, and green olives!

ingredients

2 (8 ounce) cans tomato sauce

1 lemon, peeled, halved, seeds removed

2 tablespoons prepared horseradish

2 teaspoons Worcestershire sauce

8 dashes hot sauce

1 teaspoon ground black pepper

¼ teaspoon celery salt

¾ cup vodka

4 cups ice

6 celery stalks, for garnish

directions

1. Place all ingredients, except for the ice, into the 40-ounce Processor Bowl in the order listed.

2. PULSE until smooth, using long pulses. Divide Bloody Mary over 6 glasses of ice and garnish with a celery stalk.

PREP TIME: 20 minutes   COOK TIME: 30 minutes   MAKES: 12 servings   CONTAINER: 40-ounce Processor Bowl

peach muffins

The combination of low-fat milk and nonfat yogurt gives these muffins the ultimate in moistness, with fewer calories!

ingredients

2 ripe peaches, quartered, pit removed

1 teaspoon lemon juice

¼ cup vegetable oil

½ cup low-fat milk

¼ cup nonfat yogurt

2 teaspoons vanilla extract

1 large egg

¾ cup sugar

1¾ cups all-purpose flour

2 teaspoons baking powder

¼ cup ground flax seeds

½ teaspoon kosher salt

directions

1. Preheat oven to 350°F. Lightly coat a 12-cup muffin pan with vegetable cooking spray; set aside.

2. Place the peaches into the 40-ounce Processor Bowl and PULSE to finely chop, using short pulses. Remove peaches and set aside.

3. Using the double dough blade, place the lemon juice, oil, milk, yogurt, vanilla, and egg into the 40-ounce Processor Bowl and BLEND until smooth.

4. Add the sugar, flour, baking powder, flax seeds, and salt and PULSE until combined, scraping bowl as needed. Do not overmix. Carefully remove the blades and fold in the chopped peaches with a spatula.

5. Scoop the mixture into the prepared muffin pan, filling ¾ full. Bake for 30 minutes or until a wooden pick inserted into the center comes out clean. Cool before serving.

PREP TIME: 10 minutes   RISE TIME: 4 hours   COOK TIME: 40 minutes   MAKES: 10 servings   CONTAINER: 40-ounce Processor Bowl

oatmeal raisin bread

A hearty artisan bread perfect for breakfast.

ingredients

¾ cup warm water (110–115°F)

1 tablespoon sugar

1 package (¼ ounce) active dry yeast

2 tablespoons vegetable oil

1 teaspoon kosher salt

1 cup unbleached bread flour

½ cup whole wheat flour

½ cup quick-cooking oats

1 cup dark raisins

directions

1. In a small bowl, place the water, sugar, and yeast. Allow to sit for 5 minutes.

2. Using the single dough blade, place the yeast mixture, oil, salt, flours, oats, and raisins and BLEND until well combined, about 20 seconds.

3. Remove the dough ball and place in a mixing bowl that has been coated with vegetable oil. Cover with plastic wrap and let sit in a warm place for 2 hours or until the dough has doubled in size.

4. Lightly coat a loaf pan with cooking spray. Form dough into a loaf and place in pan. Let rise for 2 hours or until double in size.

5. Preheat oven to 350°F. Bake for 35 to 40 minutes or until golden brown. Cool before serving.

NINJA KNOW-HOW WANT A SAVORY BREAD? INSTEAD OF RAISINS, ADD CHOPPED OLIVES AND ROSEMARY!

PREP TIME: 20 minutes   COOK TIME: 40 minutes   MAKES: 12 servings   CONTAINER: 40-ounce Processor Bowl

cheddar jalapeño corn bread

Corn is an often underappreciated but uniquely phytonutrient-rich food that provides us with a multitude of antioxidant benefits.

ingredients

1 cup low-fat milk

⅓ cup vegetable oil

1 large egg

⅓ cup sugar

1 teaspoon kosher salt

1 cup yellow cornmeal

1 cup all-purpose flour

1 teaspoon baking soda

2 jalapeños, halved, seeded

1 cup shredded cheddar cheese

½ cup fresh or canned corn kernels

directions

1. Preheat oven to 350°F. Lightly coat a 9 x 9 baking dish with vegetable cooking spray; set aside.

2. Place the milk, oil, and egg into the 40-ounce Processor Bowl and BLEND until smooth.

3. Add the sugar, salt, cornmeal, flour, baking soda, and jalapeños then PULSE until combined, using long pulses, scraping bowl as needed. Do not overmix.

4. Carefully remove the blades then fold in the cheese and corn.

5. Pour the batter into the prepared baking dish, bake for 35 to 40 minutes or until a wooden pick inserted into the center comes out clean. Cool before serving.

PREP TIME: 20 minutes   MAKES: 1 crust   CONTAINER: 40-ounce Processor Bowl

basic pie dough

A combination of butter and vegetable shortening creates the best consistency for the pie crust.

ingredients

1¼ cups all-purpose flour

½ teaspoon kosher salt

3 tablespoons cold unsalted butter, cut in ½-inch chunks

3 tablespoons cold vegetable shortening baking stick, cut in ½-inch chunks

¼ cup cold water

directions

1. Place the flour, salt, butter, and shortening into the 40-ounce Processor Bowl and PULSE 6 times, using long pulses.

2. Add the water and PULSE until combined, using short pulses. Do not overprocess.

3. Remove dough to a lightly floured work surface, gently form a ball, and then flatten to a 1-inch disk. Wrap with plastic wrap and refrigerate until needed.

NINJA KNOW-HOW   ALWAYS KEEP YOUR PIE CRUST AS COOL AS POSSIBLE. IN HOT WEATHER, MAKE YOUR PIE IN THE COOLER MORNING OR EVENING HOURS.

PREP TIME: 15 minutes COOK TIME: 40–45 minutes MAKES: 12 servings CONTAINER: 40-ounce Processor Bowl

pecan pie

Pecans are considered a super food by many as they are high in protein and low in carbohydrates. Pecans actually rank highest in antioxidant content among all nuts.

ingredients

Pie Crust, page 194

1⅓ cups pecan halves, roughly chopped

½ cup sugar

¼ cup light brown sugar

¾ cup light corn syrup

4 tablespoons unsalted butter

3 large eggs

3 tablespoons spiced rum

1 teaspoon vanilla extract

¼ teaspoon kosher salt

directions

1. Place oven rack on bottom shelf. Preheat oven to 325°F. Roll out the dough to a 12-inch diameter and place into a 9-inch pie dish.

2. Place the chopped pecans into the pie crust; set aside.

3. In a medium saucepot place both sugars, corn syrup, and butter and cook over low heat, stirring constantly until sugar dissolves and butter melts. Remove from heat, and cool to room temperature.

4. In the 40-ounce Processor Bowl, place the cooled sugar mixture, eggs, rum, vanilla, and salt and BLEND until combined.

5. Pour filling into prepared pie crust and bake for 40 to 45 minutes or until pie is set. Let pie cool completely before serving.

NINJA KNOW-HOW | SUBSTITUTE 1 TEASPOON RUM EXTRACT AND A PINCH OF CINNAMON AND ALLSPICE FOR THE SPICED RUM IF DESIRED.

PREP TIME: 15 minutes   COOK TIME: 10–12 minutes   MAKES: 24 cookies   CONTAINER: 40-ounce Processor Bowl

gluten-free cranberry oaties

Cranberries mixed with the coconut is a win-win in these gluten-free cookies!

ingredients

½ cup coconut oil

1 egg

½ teaspoon vanilla extract

⅓ cup packed brown sugar

⅓ cup granulated sugar

1¼ cups King Arthur Flour® gluten-free blend

½ cup almond meal

½ cup gluten-free oats

¼ cup unsweetened, shredded coconut

½ teaspoon baking soda

1 teaspoon kosher salt

½ teaspoon ground cinnamon

½ cup dried cranberries

directions

1. Preheat oven to 350°F. Place the double dough blade into the 40-ounce Processor Bowl. Add the coconut oil, egg, vanilla, brown sugar, and granulated sugar. PULSE 3 times, then run continuously for 15 seconds to cream together the ingredients. Scrape down the sides.

2. In a medium bowl, combine the flour, almond meal, oats, coconut, baking soda, salt, and cinnamon and stir to combine. Add half of the dry mixture to the Processor Bowl. PULSE 3 times, then run continuously for 10 seconds. Scrape down sides, then add remaining dry mixture. Continue to BLEND another 15 seconds until dough is evenly combined.

3. Add the cranberries to the Processor Bowl and PULSE 10 times, using short pulses, until cranberries are evenly dispersed throughout dough.

4. Spoon tablespoon-sized cookie dough onto parchment-lined cookie sheets, about 2 inches apart. Bake for 10 to 12 minutes until just golden. Cookies will be very soft upon oven removal but will set up within 5 minutes of resting.

PREP TIME: 20 minutes   **COOK TIME:** 1 hour   **MAKES:** 12 servings   **CONTAINER:** 40-ounce Processor Bowl

apple bundt cake

The apples and orange juice make this bundt cake healthier than the plain alternative.

ingredients

4 green apples, peeled, cored, diced

2 large eggs

1 cup plus 4 teaspoons sugar, divided

½ cup vegetable oil

⅓ cup orange juice

2 teaspoons vanilla extract

2 cups all-purpose flour

1 teaspoon baking powder

¼ teaspoon kosher salt

2 teaspoons ground cinnamon

directions

1. Preheat oven to 350°F. Grease a Bundt pan with vegetable cooking spray; set aside.

2. Using the double dough hook, place the eggs, 1 cup sugar, oil, orange juice, and vanilla in the 40-ounce Processor Bowl and BLEND until well mixed and sugar is dissolved.

3. Add the flour, baking powder, and salt and BLEND until combined, scraping sides as needed.

4. Pour the batter into the prepared Bundt pan and bake for approximately 1 hour or until a knife inserted into cake comes out clean.

5. Let the cake cool for at least 1 hour before removing from pan.

PREP TIME: 10 minutes   COOK TIME: 25 minutes   MAKES: 12 servings   CONTAINER: 40-ounce Processor Bowl

chocolate espresso cake

Espresso enhances chocolate's rich, deep flavor, making this cake the perfect dessert for chocolate lovers. A simple swap of milk and oil makes this a better-for-you dessert.

ingredients

½ cup low-fat milk

½ cup coconut oil, melted

½ cup water

4 large eggs

2 tablespoons instant espresso coffee

1 (3.9 ounce) package chocolate fudge pudding mix

1 (16.5 ounce) box dark chocolate fudge cake mix

Light Cream Cheese Frosting, optional, page 203

directions

1. Preheat oven to 350°F. Lightly spray the bottom of a 9x13-inch baking pan with vegetable cooking spray; set aside.

2. Place all ingredients, except for the frosting, into the 40-ounce Processor Bowl in the order listed and PULSE until smooth, using long pulses.

3. Pour batter into the prepared pan. Bake for 25 minutes or until a toothpick inserted in the center comes out clean. Cool completely before frosting, if desired.

BAKED GOODS & DESSERTS

cream cheese sugar strudel

An easy recipe that can be made from scratch—use low-fat cream cheese as a healthy option.

ingredients

1 pie dough recipe, page 194

1 (8 ounce) package low-fat cream cheese

1 teaspoon ground cinnamon

½ cup sugar

1 large egg plus 1 tablespoon water, beaten

1 cup confectioners' sugar

2 tablespoons milk

directions

1. Take the pie dough out of the refrigerator 15 to 20 minutes prior to assembly.

2. Place the cream cheese, cinnamon, and sugar into the 40-ounce Processor Bowl and BLEND until smooth, scraping bowl as needed.

3. To assemble the strudels, place the pie dough on a lightly floured surface and roll both doughs into a 9x13-inch pan, about ⅛-inch thick. Cut each piece into thirds, which will form eighteen 3x4-inch rectangles.

4. Brush nine of the rectangles with egg wash and place a tablespoon of the filling in the middle of each rectangle, keeping a 1-inch border around it. Place a second rectangle on top and press all sides to seal. Cut slits into the tops of each filled rectangle with a small knife. Refrigerate for 30 minutes.

5. Preheat oven to 350°F. Bake for 25 minutes or until golden brown. Cool.

6. Combine confectioners' sugar and milk in a mixing bowl. Spread glaze on top of each strudel.

NINJA KNOW-HOW — TRY DIFFERENT STRUDEL FILLINGS— FRUIT, NUTS, OR SAVORY.

BAKED GOODS & DESSERTS

carrot cake

A healthier and easy spin to a timeless treat! No oils or fats added!!

ingredients

2 medium carrots, peeled, cut in
2-inch chunks

1 cup water

½ cup unsweetened apple sauce

4 large eggs

1 (15.25 ounce) box carrot cake mix

Light Cream Cheese Frosting,
page 203

directions

1. Preheat oven to 325°F. Lightly spray the bottom of a 9 x 13 baking pan with vegetable cooking spray; set aside.

2. Place the carrots into the 40-ounce Processor Bowl and PULSE until chopped small, using short pulses.

3. Add remaining ingredients, except for frosting, and blend until ingredients are mixed well.

4. Pour batter into the prepared pan. Bake for 25 minutes or until a toothpick inserted in the center comes out clean. Cool completely before frosting, if desired.

PREP TIME: 5 minutes   MAKES: 1½ cups   CONTAINER: 40-ounce Processor Bowl

light cream cheese frosting

Using lower fat cream cheese and Greek yogurt makes this a lighter delighter!

ingredients

12 ounces low-fat cream cheese

3 tablespoons nonfat Greek yogurt

2 teaspoons vanilla extract

1 cup powdered sugar

directions

1. Place all ingredients into the 40-ounce Processor Bowl in the order listed.

2. PULSE until smooth, using long pulses.

NINJA KNOW-HOW ADD THE ZEST OF A LEMON, LIME OR ORANGE, OR A DROP OF YOUR FAVORITE EXTRACT, LIKE ALMOND OR PEPPERMINT TO CREATE DIFFERENT FLAVOR COMBINATIONS!

PREP TIME: 15 minutes   COOK TIME: 9–12 minutes   MAKES: 24 cookies   CONTAINER: 40-ounce Processor Bowl

chocolate chip cookies

This is truly a one bowl prep for a classic favorite—easy clean up!

ingredients

1 cup + 2 tablespoons all-purpose flour

½ teaspoon baking soda

½ teaspoon salt 1 stick unsalted butter, softened

1 large egg

½ teaspoon vanilla extract

¼ cup + 2 tablespoons granulated sugar

¼ cup + 2 tablespoons packed brown sugar

¾ cup semi-sweet chocolate morsels

directions

1. Preheat oven to 350°F. In a medium bowl, combine the flour, baking soda, and salt; set aside.

2. Using the double dough blade into the 40-ounce Processor Bowl. Add the softened butter, egg, vanilla, granulated sugar, and brown sugar then BLEND continuously for 30 seconds, until creamed. Scrape down the sides. Add the flour mixture to the Processor Bowl and PULSE 5 times. Remove the lid and scrape down the sides.

3. BLEND continuously for another 30 seconds, until incorporated well.

4. Remove the dough blade and add the chocolate chips to the Processor Bowl. Using a wooden spoon, stir in the chocolate chips.

5. Drop the cookie batter by the tablespoon onto nonstick cookie trays, 2 inches apart. Bake for 9 to 12 minutes until golden brown. Serve warm with a glass of milk!

NINJA KNOW-HOW   ADD YOUR OWN SPIN BY ADDING WALNUTS, DRIED FRUIT, OR EVEN CINNAMON.

PREP TIME: 5 minutes   COOK TIME: 5 minutes   MAKES: 1 serving   CONTAINER: 40-ounce Processor Bowl

lemon bars

Everyone loves tangy lemon bars. These are easy to make with your Food Processor Bowl.

ingredients

1 cup (2 sticks) unsalted butter, softened

2 cups sugar, divided

2⅓ cups all-purpose flour, divided

4 large eggs

⅔ cup freshly squeezed lemon juice

Confectioners' sugar to dust

directions

1. Preheat oven to 350°F.

2. Using the dough blade, place the butter, ½ cup sugar, and 2 cups flour into the Processor Bowl. PULSE, using long pulses, until dough comes together. Press dough into the bottom of an ungreased 9x13-inch baking dish. Bake for 15 minutes or until firm and golden in color. Cool for 10 minutes.

3. Place the eggs, 1½ cups sugar, ⅓ cup flour, and lemon juice into the Processor Bowl. Blend until smooth and sugar is dissolved. Pour mixture over the baked crust.

4. Bake for 20 to 23 minutes. They will firm as they cool.

5. Cool completely, and then dust with confectioners' sugar.

PREP TIME: 5 minutes   MAKES: 4 servings   CONTAINER: 40-ounce Processor Bowl

berry frozen yogurt

The perfect healthy dessert filled with fruit, plus protein with lower fat and calories than ice cream.

ingredients

2½ cups frozen raspberries

1 tablespoon stevia

1⅓ cups low-fat raspberry kefir

directions

1. Place all ingredients into the 40-ounce Processor Bowl in the order listed.

2. PULSE until smooth, using long pulses.

lemon strawberry sorbet

It is so easy to make this almost-instant sorbet with your Nutri Ninja®.

ingredients

3 cups frozen strawberries

1½ cups lemonade

directions

1. Place all ingredients into the 40-ounce Processor Bowl in the order listed.

2. BLEND until smooth.

PREP TIME: 5 minutes   MAKES: 3 servings   CONTAINER: 40-ounce Processor Bowl

hawaiian ice cream

Take a guilt-free trip to the tropics with this cold and creamy dessert.

ingredients

1½ cups frozen mango chunks

½ cup frozen pineapple chunks

1 cup canned lite coconut milk, cold

¼ cup coconut water, cold

directions

1. Add all ingredients to the 40-ounce Processor Bowl in the order listed above.

2. PULSE 5 times then BLEND continuously for 45 seconds, until smooth and creamy.

NINJA KNOW-HOW — TOP WITH YOUR FAVORITE NUTS AND COCONUT.

PREP TIME: 15 minutes   **MAKES:** 4 servings   **CONTAINER:** 40-ounce Processor Bowl

chocolate avocado mousse

....

Avocado is a healthy, simple swap for this delicious dessert!

ingredients

2 small ripe bananas, halved

2 ripe avocados, pitted, quartered, peeled

¼ cup chocolate sauce

Juice of ½ an orange

2 tablespoons cocoa powder

directions

1. Place all ingredients into the 40-ounce Processor Bowl in the order listed. BLEND until smooth, scraping down the sides of the bowl as needed.

2. Place mousse into an airtight container and refrigerate until chilled.

NINJA KNOW-HOW

REPLACE THE CHOCOLATE SAUCE WITH 2 OUNCES MELTED DARK CHOCOLATE FOR A HEALTHIER BOOST.

PREP TIME: 5 minutes   MAKES: 2 servings   CONTAINER: 40-ounce Processor Bowl

chocolate malt

Let this milkshake bring you back to the days of the classic soda-fountain, malt shops, and drugstores.

ingredients

2 cups chocolate ice cream

1½ cups milk

1 tablespoon chocolate syrup

2 tablespoons malted milk powder

2 ice cubes

directions

1. Place all ingredients into the 40-ounce Processor Bowl in the order listed.

2. BLEND until smooth.

PREP TIME: 5 minutes   MAKES: 4 servings   CONTAINER: 40-ounce Processor Bowl

peach ice cream

This fresh, 3-ingredient dessert is so easy to make, without the need of an ice cream maker! It will be a family favorite time and time again.

ingredients

2½ cups frozen peach slices

1 tablespoon fresh lime juice

3 tablespoons sugar

1 cup low-fat milk

directions

1. Place all ingredients into the 40-ounce Processor Bowl in the order listed.

2. PULSE until smooth, using long pulses.

NINJA
KNOW-HOW | FEEL FREE TO USE YOUR FAVORITE MILK FOR THIS RECIPE, INCLUDING DAIRY-FREE OPTIONS LIKE ALMOND OR COCONUT MILK.

PREP TIME: 5 minutes   MAKES: 4 servings   CONTAINER: 40-ounce Processor Bowl

mango creamsicle

This is a really delicious recipe for a homemade yogurt dessert without all the calories of the commercial stuff.

ingredients

3 cups frozen mango chunks

⅓ cup nonfat yogurt

½ cup coconut water

1 tablespoon honey

directions

1. Place all ingredients into the 40-ounce Processor Bowl in the order listed.

2. BLEND until smooth.

NINJA KNOW-HOW — FOR A DELICIOUS VARIATION, SWAP FROZEN PEACHES FOR THE MANGO.

index

index

NUTRI
NINJA 2-in-1

Healthy & Delicious
Made Easy

150 Recipes from healthy nutrient-rich juices to delicious meal making